For the
Love of Music

An Inspirational Daily Devotional for Music Lovers,
Musicians, Music Teachers and Music Students

Don and Delayna Beattie

Dedicated to Our Parents
Donna and Russel Staples and
Margaret and Paul Beattie

Foreword

In the pages of this Devotional are writings that have deeply inspired and shaped our musical, educational and spiritual lives. Having been collecting these types of writings for nearly 50 years, this collection has truly been a lifetime in the making and will continue to inspire our lives. So wishing to share these writings with all those who love music, we felt that a Daily Devotional would be the best format in which to do so. We enjoy reading devotionals and a short reading at the beginning of our day often helps set the tone for the day in a positive way. May this Devotional serve you well in a similar way.

While many write with great insight on the subjects of how we think, how we learn, how we love and how we live, we have found such inspiration in the most unexpected places. The few words on a wall hanging in our grandmother's kitchen, *"You are Thy Thoughts,"* found a permanent place in our hearts. May the writings of this devotional serve as daily inspiration for you and find a meaningful place in your hearts and thoughts regarding music and life. In our lives, we continue to learn so much about the gift, the power, the meaning and the learning of music. At the same time, the great pianist and teacher, Franz Liszt, said that in playing the piano, *"we so easily become preoccupied with the manual work of playing that we forget to rise again to the source."* To take his thought a step further, we have often found ourselves so preoccupied with the *"manual work"* of life that we forget to *"rise to the source"* of life. Thanks in part to these writings, we are able to continually renew our appreciation and gratitude for the gift of life, the gift of love and in the case of this Devotional, the gift of music.

In a word, music is a *"gift"* and as another has expressed *"the universal language of mankind."* Experiencing this universal gift, in the hands of children and great artists alike, has inspired us beyond words. We have seen music lift the soul, give voice to the heart, foster an ever expanding vision of the gift of life and even save lives. We need music and we need the continuing guidance of those great artists in our midst and those who have come before to show us the way to *"the source."* In the words of the great German composer, Robert Schumann, *"when you think you have an original idea, think again."* There is no doubt in our minds that the *"origin"* of so many deeply meaningful thoughts in our lives have come from others. May this devotional, comprised of the words of many others, bring you an ever deepening understanding of love for music and for life.

Don and Delayna Beattie
March, 2017

Don and Delayna Beattie

Throughout the course of their careers as musicians and teachers, Don and Delayna have touched the lives of thousands of children and adults throughout the world. Between them, they have performed, presented workshops and hosted music festivals in all 50 of the United States, Canada, Austria and Germany. They are published authors, composers and recording artists with Warner Bros. and Edition Has Music Publishing Co. with Don having presented 200 piano teacher workshops throughout North America for G. Henle Verlag music publishers of Munich, Germany. Their four volume "*Beethoven Library of Piano Works,*" published by Warner Bros, is acclaimed and Don's "*Please Grant my Wish for Peace,*" performed by choirs for President George Herbert W. Bush at the Kennedy Center and for President Bill Clinton at the White House, was reviewed in the Choral Journal as "*a miniature masterpiece of our time.*"

Both Don and Delayna have been active as presenters with the Music Teachers National Association (MTNA), Music Educators National Conference (MENC) and conferences of the World Piano Pedagogy Conference (WPPC) where Don served notably as the Master of Ceremonies for many years. Don's founding of the "*Beethoven Society for Pianists,*" and subsequent leadership with Delayna, created internationally renowned Beethoven Festivals that brought young pianists, teachers, great artists and audiences together in a new way. The Society was founded in 1984 at Southern Illinois University Carbondale where Don served as Professor of Piano and Director of Piano Pedagogy for thirty years. Some of the greatest artists in the world became frequent guests of the Society with Society Chapters formed throughout the United States, Canada and Germany. The Society also inspired founding of the "*Beethoven Piano Society of Europe*" with Alfred Brendel serving as their first President.

Don holds undergraduate and graduate music degrees from the University of Colorado, Boulder as well as PhD studies in Educational Psychology at Southern Illinois University Carbondale. Following music studies throughout her youth and college, Delayna distinguished herself for leadership with the Iowa State and National Music Teachers Association and as a dedicated and creative teacher of young people as an independent music teacher. Together, they are known as a joyful and extraordinary teaching team with their teaching, performances, festivals, church music and publishing continuing. They have been blessed as parents with four children and four grandchildren that live throughout the United States. From this Devotional, you will find the words of Frederick William Faber who said "*There are souls in this world which have the gift of finding joy everywhere and leaving it behind them when they go.*" As people, musicians and teachers, this may best describe Don and Delayna Beattie.

Authors of These Inspirational Writings

ADAMS, John, AGEE, James, ARRAU Claudio, ASSOCIATED Press, ASSOCIATION, National Child Welfare, BACH, Carl Philipp Emanuel, BACH, Johann Sebastian, BARTH, Karl, BARTOK, Bela, BEAUDELAIRE, Charles, BEATTIE, Don and Delayna, BEETHOVEN, Ludwig van, BERLIOZ, Hector, BIBLE, The, BLOCH, Ernest, BRAHMS, Johannes, BROWN, Sir Thomas, BURNE-JONES, Sir Edward Coley, CANIN, Martin, CARLYLE, Thomas, CASALS, Pablo, CHAVEZ, Carlos, CHIAPUSSO, Jan, CHOPIN, Frederic, CHRYSOSTOM, St. John, CONFUCIUS, COOPER, Martin, COPLAND, Aaron, CRANKSHAW, Edward, CZERNY, Carl, DANTE, DA VINCI, Leonardo, DE CHARDIN, Pierre Teilhard, DEBUSSY, Claude, DENVER, John, DIEPENBROCK, Alphons, DRAKE, Kenneth, DUKAS, Paul, DYKE, Henry Jackson van, EDWARDS, Elaine, EMERSON, Ralph Waldo, FABER, Frederick William, FLAXMAN, Andrew, FREUD, Sigmund, GERIG, Reginald, GERSHWIN, George, GILMAN, Lawrence, GOETHE, Johann Wolfgang von, GOULD, Glenn, GRAHAM, Billy, GROVE, Sir George, GUEVARA, JR., Dr. Alfredo Che, HANDEL, G. F., HENDRIX, Jimi, HOFFMANN, E.T.A., HOROWITZ, Vladimir, HSU, Madeleine, HUGO, Victor, INMAN, Allan C., IVES, Charles, JEFFERSON, Thomas, KEMPFF, Wilhelm, KRAUS, Lili, LANIER, Sydney, LEIBNITZ, Gottfried Wilhelm, LINCOLN, Abraham, LISZT, Franz, LONGFELLOW, Henry Wadsworth, MAHLER, Gustav, MANNES, David, MASLOW, Abraham, MENDELSSOHN, Felix, MIKULI, Karol, MILAY, Edna St. Vincent, MOLIERE, Jean-Baptiste Poquelin, MOZART, Wolfgang Amadeus, NEEFE, Christian Gottlob, NEWMAN, Ernest, NIETZSCHE, Freidrich, NIN, Anais, ORGA, Artes, OSTEEN, Joel, PADEREWSKI, Ignace, PAUER, Ernst, PLATO, POE, Edgar Allan, PORTER, Nicholas, PYTHAGORAS, RACHMANINOFF, Sergei, RAVEL, Maurice, RICHTER, Jean Paul, RIES, Ferdinand, RIMBAUD, J. Arthur, RODMAN, Selden, ROES, Paul, ROLLAND, Romain, RUSSELL, A.J., SAND, George, SCHILLER, Friedrich, SCHINDLER, Anton, SCHLOSSER, Louis, SCHNABEL, Artur, SCHONBERG, Harold, SCHOPENHAUER, Arthur, SCHUBERT, Franz, SCHULTZ, Charles, SCHUMANN, Robert, SCHWEITZER, Albert, SESSIONS, Roger, SEVILLE, Isidore of, SEYFRIED, Ignaz von, SHAKESPEARE, William, SHANKHAR, Ravi, SITWELL, Sir Sacheverell, SPENSER, Edmund, STORM, Mel, STUMPFF, Johann Andreas, SULLIVAN, J.W.N., TAYLOR, James, TCHAIKOVSKY, Peter Ilich, THOREAU, Henry David, TIGHE, Sister Alice Eugene, TREITSCHKE, Georg Friedrich, TURNER, W.J., VAN PRAAGH, James, WAGNER, Richard, WARREN, Rick, WASHINGTON, George, WEBER, Carl Maria, WHITEHEAD, Alfred North, WHONE, Herbert, WRIGHT, Frank Lloyd, YOGI, Maharishi Mahesh, ZAPPA, Frank

Don and Delayna Beattie

January

Our Shih Tzu LE (pronounced Ellie) in Jewell, Iowa

January 1

"Everything is music for the born musician. Everything that throbs, or moves, or stirs, or palpitates – sunlit summer days, nights when the wind howls, flickering light, the twinkling of the stars, storms, the song of birds, the buzzing of insects, the murmuring of trees, voice, loved or loathed, familiar fireside sound, a creaking door, blood moving in the veins in the silence of the night – everything that is
is music; all that is needed is that it should be heard."

Romain Rolland
French Writer (1866-1944)

January 2

"When the artist is vigorous enough to delve down to the great laws of the general life and the essential rhythms of the soul, the masterpiece (Beethoven's Symphony No. 3 "Eroica") of the individual genius becomes, without effort or intention on his part, the natural expression of all humanity. And I affirm that this oneness is the highest harmony that can be realized on earth. Beethoven has accomplished it in the 'Eroica.'"

Romain Rolland
Author of "Beethoven, the Creator"

January 3

"There need be no other reason for song and music other than to praise and thank God. An amazing thing happens when we offer praise and thanksgiving to God. When we give God enjoyment, our own hearts are filled with joy. Herein lies the real purpose of music."

A.J. Russell
London Newspaper Editor (1861-1945)
Editor, "God Calling"

January 4

In conversation with Johann Wenzel Tomaschek in 1814, Beethoven said, "I was formerly inconsiderate and hasty in the expression of my opinions, and thereby I made enemies. Now I pass judgment on no one, and, indeed, for the reason that I do not wish to do any one harm." In his diary, Beethoven wrote, "The just man must be able to suffer injustice without deviating in the least from the right course."

Ludwig van Beethoven
German Composer (1770-1827)

January 5

"Whether the angels play only Bach in praising God I am not quite sure; I am sure however, than *en famille* (as a family), they play Mozart."

Karl Barth
Swiss Theologian (1886-1968)

January 6

"Music excavates Heaven."

Charles Beaudelaire
French Poet (1821-1867)

January 7

"On September 11, 1777 (exactly 180 years before the tragedy of September 11, 2001), the Continental Congress voted to spend three hundred thousand dollars to buy copies of the Bible to be distributed throughout the colonies. This was widely accepted, of course."

Billy Graham
American Evangelist (1918 -)
Author of "Where I Am"

January 8

"The roots of our educational institutions were based on faith in God. Harvard University was founded in 1636. In John Harvard's bequest to the school, he left several rules and precepts that were to be observed by the college bearing his name. The second rule states: 'Let every student be plainly instructed, and earnestly pressed to consider well, the main end of his life and studies is, to know God and Jesus Christ which is eternal life . . . and therefore to lay Christ in the bottom as the only foundation of all sound knowledge and learning. And seeing the Lord only gives wisdom, let everyone seriously set himself by prayer in secret to seek it of him.' Mr. Harvard wanted higher education to be a place where people would come to study the Bible and acknowledge Christ as Lord and Savior."

Billy Graham

January 9

"I must study politics and war that my sons may have liberty to study mathematics and philosophy...in order to give their children a right to study painting, poetry, and music."

John Adams
United States President (1735-1826)

January 10

"When I open my eyes, I must sigh, for what I look upon is contrary to my religion, and I must despise the world which never divines that music is a greater revelation than the whole of wisdom and philosophy."

Ludwig van Beethoven

January 11

In 1909, C.C. Birchard & Company of Boston published the Master-Musician Series as "A Course of Studies in the Lives and Works of the Classic Composers." From their volume on Beethoven it reads, "In a broad sense, Beethoven was deeply reverent as is attested by the following motto or creed which he kept before him on his writing desk,

'I Am that which is,
I Am all that is, that was and that shall be.
No mortal man hath lifted My veil.
He is alone by Himself and to Him alone
do all things owe their existence.'"

Beethoven's friend, Anton Schindler, reported the same story saying that Beethoven kept this inscription framed and constantly before him or under the glass of his writing desk. These words have their source in the Bible as God spoke to Moses concerning God's name. In the summer of 1814, Beethoven simply wrote in a conversation book to a friend, 'Socrates and Jesus were my exemplars.'"

Anton Schindler
Violinist, Teacher and Author (1795-1864)
Author of "The Life of Beethoven"

January 12

Beethoven truly believed music was his life force and a source of comfort and joy to all. From Selden Rodman's book, *"The Heart of Beethoven,"* we are indebted to Felix Mendelssohn for the following story.

"The A Major Piano Sonata, opus 101, completed in 1816, first of his characteristic works of the Third Period, was dedicated to the pianist, Dorothea von Ertmann. Long after Beethoven's death, the aged Baroness told how that in the months preceding the writing of this sonata, she had lost her last child and was on the verge of what we now call a nervous breakdown. Hearing this, Beethoven invited her to his room and said: 'We will now talk to each other in tones,' and he improvised on his piano for more than an hour - something he hadn't done in years.

Here was Beethoven, the intensely human being, who comforted his pupil, Baroness Dorothea von Ertmann, in the loss of her child by saying not a word, but by playing the piano from his heart to hers uninterruptedly for over an hour. 'He told me everything,' she confided to Mendelssohn, 'and at last brought me comfort.' Beethoven's improvisation that day became the basis for the first movement of his A Major Sonata, opus 101, and with its compressed style, its directions for expressiveness in German rather than Italian, its abrupt changes of mood, its suggestions of unearthly joy and its tremendous fugal finale, point the way to the ultimate Beethoven.'"

Felix Mendelssohn
German Composer, Pianist, Teacher (1809-1847)

January 13

"Which of the two powers, love or music, is able to lift man to the sublimest heights? It is a great question, but it seems to me that one might answer it thus: Love cannot express the idea of music, while music may give an idea of love. Why separate the one from the other? They are the two wings of the soul."

Hector Berlioz
French Composer (1803-1869)

January 14

"All true and deeply felt music, whether sacred or profane, journeys to
heights where art and religion can always meet."

Albert Schweitzer
French Theologian, Philosopher and Musician (1875-1965)

January 15

"The only really happy people
are those who have learned how to serve."

Albert Schweitzer

January 16

"I believe that some day, we shall be weary of this daily, miserable
struggle and that a little true love will be born in the withered hearts of
men. Perhaps, after our hatred, kindled only by a few, there will come
one of those cleansing revolutions that will shake the world on it's
foundations and sweep away the poisonous vapors. Perhaps, then, a new
life will rise up and with it something of youth and virtue and joy while
the old limping religions, the gods in whom no one believes, will be
swept away with the ruins. A little fraternity, a little love, a little gladness
will gleam on the face of the world, and catch up the hearts of men in
one impulse, in one rhythm and for these new hearts, there will be need
to be new songs."

Ernest Bloch
American Composer (1880-1959)

January 17

"Then I heard every creature in heaven and on earth and under the earth
and on the sea, and all that is in them singing: To Him who sits on the
throne and to the Lamb be praise and honor and glory and power, for
ever and ever!"

Revelation 5:13
The Bible

January 18

"Each second that we live is a new and unique moment of the universe, a
moment that never was before and never will be again. And what do we
teach our children in school? We teach them that two and two make four
and that Paris is the capital of France. When will we also help to teach
them who and what and why they are? You are a marvel. You are
unique. In all of the world there is no other child exactly like you. In the
millions of years that have passed there has never been a child like you.
Look at your body – what a wonder it is! - your legs, your arms, your

fingers, the way you move! You may become a Shakespeare, a Michelangelo, a Beethoven You have the capacity for anything. Yes, you are a marvel. And when you grow up, can you then harm another who is, like you, a marvel? We must cherish one another. We must all work to make this world worthy of its children."

Pablo Casals
Cellist, Conductor and Humanitarian (1876-1973)

January 19
"Music which does not contain an idea is not music."

Frederic Chopin
Polish Pianist and Composer (1810-1849)

January 20
"If we let life overwhelm us, and we go around worried, stressed out, and locked in self-pity, we are not only affected mentally; we are also affected physically. The stress and worry weaken our immune system, which then can't fight off sickness and disease the way God created it to. The Scripture says, 'The joy of the Lord is your strength.' Joy is an emotion, and yet it creates something physical. It creates strength. When you're in tough times, you have to shake off the worry, shake off the self-pity, shake off the disappointment. Get your joy back." (and listen to Beethoven's Symphony No. 9, opus 125 Ode to Joy.)

Joel Osteen
American Evangelist (1963)
Author of "The Power of I Am"

January 21
Sir Edward Coley Burne-Jones wrote to Oscar Wilde that "the more materialistic science becomes, the more angels shall I paint. Their wings are my protest in favor of the immortality of the soul."

Sir Edward Coley Burne-Jones
English Artist (1833-1898)

January 22
"Music is well said to be the speech of angels; in fact, nothing among the utterances allowed to man is felt to be so divine. It brings us near to the infinite."

Thomas Carlyle
Scottish Essayist (1795-1881)

January 23

"From every indication we have, Chopin must have been a superb teacher. One morning, he played from memory fourteen Preludes and Fugues of Bach. 'When I am about to give a concert, I close my doors for a time and play Bach.' In his last year Chopin began work on a proposed method book, a project which unfortunately he was unable to complete."

Frederic Chopin

January 24

"Music rises from the human heart. When the emotions are touched, they are expressed in sound, and when the sounds take definite forms, we have music. Therefore the music of a peaceful and prosperous country is quiet and joyous, and the government is orderly; the music of a country in turmoil shows dissatisfaction and anger, and the government is chaotic; and the music of a destroyed country show sorrow and remembrance of the past and the people are distressed. Thus we see music and government are directly connected with one another."

Confucius
Chinese Philosopher (551-479 BC)

January 25

"The poem gives expression to our heart, the song gives expression to our voice, and the dance gives expression to our movements. These three arts take their rise from the human soul, and then are given further expression by means of the musical instrument."

Confucius

January 26

"Do you know that our soul is composed of harmony."

Leonardo da Vinci
Painter and Renaissance Man (1452-1519)

January 27

Birthday of Wolfgang Amadeus Mozart (1756-1791)
"In 1770, Mozart, on tour with his father in Italy, gave an exhibition, for it was an exhibition rather than a concert, even though it was 'reviewed,' at the Reale Academia in Mantua. At the Academia there were several professional musicians, and they prepared the program.

First, one of the boy's symphonies was played. Then he was soloist in a piano concerto that he had to read at sight from manuscript. Then he was supplied with a solo sonata which he not only had to read at sight but also supply with variations; and, that done, he had to transpose the work to another key. Then he had to compose an aria on the spot, to words given him, sing it himself and accompany himself on the clavier.

Following this, the concertmaster of the orchestra gave Mozart a theme, and Mozart had to improvise a sonata from it. Then he had to improvise a strict fugue. Then he had to play the violin in a trio. Finally he conducted, from the clavier, one of his own symphonies. Mozart was fourteen years old at the time. A few years later he was to be instrumental in launching the piano on it's decisive career. He was the first of the great pianists."

Harold Schonberg
American Music Critic and Journalist (1915-2003)
Author of "The Great Pianists from Mozart to the Present"

January 28

"People make a mistake who think that my art has come easily to me. Nobody has devoted so much time and thought to compositions as I. There is not a famous master whose music I have not studied over and over."

Wolfgang Amadeus Mozart
Austrian Composer, Pianist, Conductor (1756-1791)

January 29

"All the good music has already been written
by people with wigs and stuff."

Frank Zappa
American Musician and Composer (1940-1993)

January 30

"O Mozart, immortal Mozart, how many, how infinitely many inspiring
suggestions of a finer, better life you left in our souls."

From Franz Schubert's Diary, 1816
Franz Schubert
Austrian Composer (1797-1828)

January 31

Birthday of Franz Schubert (1797-1828)

"I am in the world only for the purpose of composing."

Franz Schubert

February

In the Great Smoky Mountains National Park

February 1

"Look up on a starry night, and you will see the majesty and power of an infinite Creator. Recently I saw a report about some new discoveries in astronomy. It stated that astronomers now believe there may be as many as 140 billion galaxies in the known universe, some more than eleven billion light-years away and each containing at least several hundred billion stars . . . Scientists point out that there are more stars in the universe than grains of sand on the planet Earth . . . We can't begin to imagine such distances or quantities . . . I read an article pointing out that our bodies contain about ten thousand trillion cells, each one containing a strand of our individual DNA, an unimaginable number . . . Even when we look within ourselves, we detect God's handiwork. Our creativity, our inner sense of right and wrong, our ability to love and to reason - all bear witness to the fact the God created us in His image."

Billy Graham

February 2

In the year that Beethoven finished the Seventh Symphony he wrote: "Almighty One, in the woods I am blessed. Happy everyone in the woods. You speak through every tree, O God! What glory in the woodland! On the heights is peace – peace to serve Him."

Ludwig van Beethoven

February 3

Birthday of Felix Mendelssohn (1809-1847)

In conversation with Neate, Beethoven said:
"I always have a picture in my mind when composing,
and follow its lines."

Ludwig van Beethoven

February 4

"He who holds to the bonds of this world
has not yet heard all music."

Dante
Italian Poet (1265-1321)

February 5

"So is music an asylum. It takes us out of the actual and whispers to us dim secrets that startle our wonder as to who we are, and for what, whence and whereto. All the great interrogatories, like questioning angels, float in on its waves of sound."

Ralph Waldo Emerson
Essayist and Philosopher (1803-1882)

February 6

"The principal problem in interpretation is coming as close as possible to what we know to be the intentions of the composer; and from that basis, taking your own flight of imagination. Interpretation is on the one hand serving the intentions of the composer and on the other hand putting the interpreter's own blood and personality into the realization of the text. These two things must the balanced."

Claudio Arrau
Concert pianist (1903-1991)

February 7

"I would advise young artists to remember that as individuals, as interpreters, they are unique. They have the small, big, or deep message which is their very own. The most important thing then is to fulfill themselves as personalities, in this case as creative personalities – to try not to please but, as the saying goes, 'to do their own thing.'"

Claudio Arrau

February 8

"I played all the Bach keyboard work in twelve recitals in Berlin in 1935. Afterwards, I decided that the piano itself causes a performer to bring something to Bach that doesn't belong, that somehow sounds a little too worldly. Not that Bach doesn't have emotions, but they are different emotions – usually on the spiritual side. Take the *"Chromatic Fantasy"* – it's like a dialogue with God, with the Infinite. It is music for the glory of God..."

Claudio Arrau

February 9

"In his late works, Beethoven arrives at a metaphysical language of expression where trills become a trembling of the soul."

Claudio Arrau

February 10

"Gather impressions but don't hurry to note them down for music has this over painting that it can bring together all manner of variations of colour and light. It is a point that is not often observed though it is quite obvious. And then, from time to time, forget music altogether. 'Practice makes perfect' is a schoolmaster's notion."

Claude Debussy
French Composer (1862-1918)

February 11

"Be it laughter or tears, feverish passion or religious ecstasy, nothing in the category of human feelings, is a stranger to music."

Paul Dukas
French Composer (1865-1935)

February 12

"...over the entrance to the Sanctuary of Apollo at Delphi was the admonition: 'Know Thyself!' The true oracle, this ancient wisdom suggest, lies within. The answers to the great human questions, public and private, are found not outside us but only through an inner journey of the seeking spirit. The crucial importance of developing self-knowledge can be best understood in the words of another ancient piece of wisdom. The Hebraic Talmud says, 'We do not see things the way they are, we see things the way we are.'"

Andrew Flaxman
American Educator

February 13

"One of the marks of a great work of art is its containment of several different layers of meaning. How much we receive from this music depends upon how much we bring to it and how carefully we pay attention to it."

Andrew Flaxman

February 14

"Music is love in search of word."

Sidney Lanier
American Musician and Poet (1842-1881)

February 15

"In a sense, any predicable is true of music: just as one may say anything of God, because, being Infinite, there is nothing He is not."

Sidney Lanier

February 16

"Although in our materialistic age art has lost this spiritual connection by becoming over-concerned with the obvious reality of life between birth and death, the Far East has always known that the roots of music lie in the spiritual world. Western culture with Pythagoras and Plato started with a similar outlook. But as Western thinking became more and more man-centered, nature has taken the place of God in much of man's devotional and artistic efforts...During the past two hundred years, this materialistic attitude grew and took hold. Most people were now so absorbed in themselves and their surroundings that they saw art as merely a matter of pleasure, rather than as having any spiritual relationship."

Andrew Flaxman

February 17

"Through the music of Mozart, we find reconciliation of beauty and pain. Peace, joy and strength are shown to be possible in the face of the most enormous emotional conflicts. The more intimately we come to know this music, the more it gives to us. It speaks directly into our hearts, meaning our 'souls,' so that we know that our true home is not merely an earthly consciousness but something deeper – a 'spiritual kingdom.'"

Andrew Flaxman

February 18

"Piano Playing: The word 'playing' is appropriate here, for the playing of an instrument must be an integral part of it; he who cannot play with it, cannot play it at all."

Robert Schumann
German Composer and Journalist (1810-1856)
Author of "On Music and Musicians"

February 19

From his collection of aphorisms in the book, *"On Music and Musicians,"* Robert Schumann wrote, "Nothing worth while can be accomplished in art without enthusiasm." From Pastor Joel Osteen's book, *"Your Best Life Now,"* "The word enthusiasm derives from the two Greek words, *en theos*, meaning 'inspired by God.' Our lives need to be inspired, infused, filled afresh with God's goodness every day. . . Who knows what would happen if each of us lived with more excitement in our eyes, with our hearts full of passion, our faces filled with enthusiasm? . . . Don't just go through the motions in life. Have some enthusiasm."

Robert Schumann and Joel Osteen

February 20

Birthday of Carl Czerny (1791-1857)
"Anything that happens in the world affects me; politics, for example, literature, people and I reflect about all these things in my own way – and these reflections then seek to find an outlet in my music. This is also the reason for which so many of my compositions are hard to understand..."

Robert Schumann

February 21

"Beethoven lived in a universe richer than ours, in some ways better than ours, and in some ways more terrible. And yet we recognize his universe and find his attitudes toward it prophetic of our own. It is indeed our own universe, but as experienced by a consciousness which is aware of aspects of which we have but dim and transitory glimpses."

J.W.N. Sullivan
Popular Science Writer and Literary Journalist (1886-1937)
Author of "Beethoven: His Spiritual Development"

February 22

"Beethoven regarded art as a way of communicating knowledge about reality. Beethoven was a firm believer in what Mr. I.A. Richard calls the 'revelation theory' of art. This is a theory which, if true, means that art has a significance very much more important than that usually attributed to it. Art must rank with science and philosophy as a way of communicating knowledge about reality."

J.W.N. Sullivan

February 23

Birthday of George Frederic Handel (1685-1759)
"There is no loftier mission than to approach the Divinity nearer than other men, and to disseminate the divine rays among mankind...You will ask me where I get my ideas. That I cannot tell you with certainty; they come unsummoned, directly, indirectly - I could seize them with my hands – out in the open air, in the woods, while walking, in the silence of the nights, early in the morning, incited by moods which are translated by the poet into words, by me into tones that sounds, and roar and storm about me until I have set them down in notes."

Ludwig van Beethoven

February 24

"Science is learning to control just about everything but man. More important than electricity, technology and medicine are the issues of the heart. Solve the problems of hate, lust, greed and prejudice - which produce social strife and ultimately war - and the world would be a different place. Our future is threatened by many dangers, but they all stem from the heart. The Bible says that the human heart is corrupt. This is why Christ came - to give new hearts to the human race." (Music awakens the heart. Music provides lessons and learning about the heart.)

Billy Graham

February 25

"And be not drunk with wine, where in is excess; but be filled with the Spirit; Speaking to yourselves in psalms and hymns and spiritual songs, singing and making melody in your heart to the Lord."

Ephesians 5:18
The Bible

February 26

"...It is at once by poetry and through poetry, of music and through music, that the soul divines what splendors shine behind the tomb..."

Edgar Allan Poe
American Poet (1809-1849)

February 27

"God sent his singers upon earth,
With songs of sadness and of mirth,
That they might touch the hearts of men,
And bring them back to heaven again."

Henry Wadsworth Longfellow
American Poet (1807-1882)

February 28

"Through music, a child enters a world of beauty, expresses his inmost self, tastes the joy of creating, widens his sympathies, develops his mind, soothes and refines his spirit and adds grace to his body."

The United States
National Child Welfare Association

February 29

Lucy: If you use your imagination, you can see lots of things in the cloud formations. What do you think you see, Linus?

Linus: Well, those clouds up there look to me like the map of the British Honduras on the Caribbean. That cloud up there looks a little like the profile of Thomas Eakins, the famous painter and sculptor and that group of clouds over there give me the impression of the stoning of Stephen. I can see the Apostle Paul standing there to one side...

Lucy: Uh, huh...That's very good. What do you see in the clouds, Charlie Brown?

Charlie Brown: Well, I was going to say I saw a ducky and a horsie, but I changed my mind!

Charles Schultz
American Cartoonist (1922-2000)

Don and Delayna Beattie

March

In St. Maarten

March 1

"Arturo Toscanini said, 'If you want to please the critics, don't play too fast and don't play too loud, and don't play too slow and don't play too soft. Don't over interpret and don't under interpret. And so the music will be boring.' You cannot play to please the critics. Instead, you must love the music. Music is five lines, with notes, some black and some white, some a little blacker. And if you play them as written, you play a typewriter machine. The music is behind the notes. The sense of music is that you have to open the box and there is the music on the other side."

Vladimir Horowitz
Concert Pianist (1903-1989)

March 2

"Chopin said, 'Sound came before the word.' When his pupils tried to imitate him, he always sent them home. First, because he wanted them to bring something of their own, even for his own compositions. And second, because he never played the same way twice. You have to improvise. I sometimes discover new things on the stage."

Vladimir Horowitz

March 3
Birthday of Frederic Chopin (1810-1849)

"Chopin advocated a cantabile approach. The musical pianist had to sing and with his singing there must be the most natural phrasing. If he failed in this regard, Mikuli quoted Chopin often repeating...that it struck him as if some one were reciting, in a language not understood by the speaker, a speech carefully learned by rote, in the course of which the speaker not only neglected the natural quantity of the syllables, but even stopped in the middle of words. The pseudo-musician, he said, shows in a similar way, by his wrong phrasing, that music is not his mother-tongue, but something foreign and incomprehensible to him, and must, like the aforesaid speaker, quite renounce the idea of making any effect upon his hearers by his delivery."

Karol Mikuli
Polish Pianist, Composer and Teacher (1819-1897)

March 4
Birthday of Antonio Vivaldi (1678-1741)

"Chopin's intensely musical nature, his incredible control of an infinite number of subtle dynamic shadings and rhythmic nuances always had a stronger appeal for the musically discerning than for the populace."

Reginald Gerig

March 5
"The emphasis by young performers seems to be on playing every note in its proper place, but without making a personal statement, showing no passionate involvement and taking no risks. It all sounds the same: slow, fast, soft, loud. But I want to hear concepts, not just notes. The emotional content of what is played must be in head and heart, not just in the fingers or on the sleeve."

Lili Kraus
Concert Pianist (1903-1986)

March 6
"In his diary, Leonardo da Vinci said that the true experience of the artist at times is so terrifying that, if the artistic vision were present in full truth to the layman, he would be so shocked that he would flee in terror. Therefore, according to Leonardo, it is the duty and sacred privilege of the creative artist to cloak his experience in the garb of love and perfection. Now this is precisely what Mozart has done, and his music has become so much a part of me that I agonize when the music turns to the minor, and I'm redeemed when it reverts to the major."

Lili Kraus

March 7

Birthday of Maurice Ravel (1875-1937)

"Great music has always been sensitive balance between the emotion and the intellect, Too much emotion and too little intellect lead to mawkish music which is revolting. On the other hand, too much intellect and too little emotion lead to the ugliness which characterized the 'modern music'. Somewhere between those two extremes lies the golden mean which composers should strive for."

Maurice Ravel
French composer (1875-1937)

March 8

Birthday of Carl Phillip Emmanuel Bach (1714-1788)

"C.P.E. Bach's fundamental artistic code was what the artist of the Renaissance had realized long before: 'All art should contain a spiritual message and must breathe it forth with an emotion so powerful that the listener, seeing it or hearing it, must perforce grasp it's real significance."

Carl Philipp Emanuel Bach
German Composer (1714-1788)

March 9

"We have a responsibility. God has entrusted you with His Life. He breathed His Breath into you. He's put gifts and talents inside of you. You have seeds of greatness. You're not just on planet Earth taking up space. You're a person of destiny. With this gift of life comes a responsibility to develop your talents, to pursue your dreams and to become who God's created you to be."

Joel Osteen

March 10

If you move the letter H from the end to the front of the word Earth, it spells Heart. We believe that God planned each "plan-it" and that we are blessed to have the gift of life on Earth to learn lessons of the Heart. When we consider the origin of the word government as "God over men," it sheds new light on our American phrase, "In God We Trust."

Don and Delayna Beattie

March 11

"I feel the capacity to care is the thing which gives
life its deepest significance."

Pablo Casals

March 12

"One of the elements that has attracted Claudio Arrau to follow his lifelong pilgrimage for truth in Beethoven's music is the feeling that it represents the highest possible level of human achievement and self-realization."

Clavier magazine, March, 1983
Claudio Arrau

March 13

"So much of what Beethoven expresses is unique; nothing like it can be found elsewhere, either in music or poetry, and yet we regard these unique states as fundamental and greatly prize them. It is as if Beethoven is the one voice that has expressed a certain region of the human soul – states of consciousness that we may call musical in the sense that they have been expressed, and perhaps can be expressed, only in music."

J.W.N. Sullivan

March 14

"The 'personality' of such a man as Beethoven is slowly developed synthetic whole. It is formed by the gradual combination of its constituent elements into an organic unity. For the development of a personality a rich and profound inner life is necessary, and for that reason, it is usually only great artists and religious teachers who impress us as being complete persons."

J.W.N. Sullivan

March 15

"The only times when I have witnessed a state approaching the brotherhood of man have been moments of music, when hundreds of hearts beat to the same rhythm and lifted to the same phrase and when all hate, all envy, all greed were washed away by the nobility of sound... to learn the language of music – or at least to respond to it – one need only an ear and a heart."

David Mannes
American Musician and Educator (1866-1959)

March 16

"Liszt and Busoni both understood that to awaken the self-educator in the pupil is the sole precept to follow."

Paul Roes

March 17

I've Found My Way
An Anthem Commissioned by the National Teachers Hall of Fame
"Pages of your book grew worn, like a rose upon a thorn,
Though the rain and storm would come,
your gentle voice warm as the sun,
Seeds you scattered on the ground, wondering if lost or found,
Looking back, your stories told, helped gardens grow and dreams unfold.
Artist, scholar, teacher, priest, all nourished by a learning feast,
Is there a place for me to sit, with thee and listen as you wonder,
Where are the children and who have the children become,
Come with me and I'll tell you a story,
like those that you once told to me.
When you hear of great discovery,
know the doors were opened with your key,
You're the one who was the first playwright,
now we're acting on the stage of life,
And it's me, thanks to thee, I can say, I've found my way.
Peering out to stars at night, everyone a child in sight,
Even now I ponder things, you said, and wonder what to sing,
Is it at the highest star, where we find out who we are,
Is it in the mountain climb, that I will find what's really mine.
Artist, scholar, teacher, priest, all nourished by a learning feast,
Is there a place for me to sit, with thee and listen as you speak,
Where do birds go when they fly, they seem to disappear on high,
Is the place where colors of autumn and winter winds blow,
The place where the rainbows go,
Come with me and I'll tell you a story,
like those that you once told to me.
When you learn of those who've gone to space,
Remember years gone by their once small face,
All the children that you watched 'til night,
Now we're running in the race of life,
People that go down in history, they were lifted up by you to see,
Parades of people that have gone before,
Once upon a time, they knocked upon your door,
Now it's me, thanks to thee, I can say, I've found my way,
It's me, thanks to thee, I feel free and I've found my way,
Thanks be to thee, I have found my way,
Thanks be to thee, I have found my way."

Donald Beattie
c. 1996. Edition HAS Music Publishing Co.

March 18

"Above all no imitation.
It is better to find for yourself, after mere suggestion on my part."

Franz Liszt
Hungarian Concert Pianist and Composer (1811-1886)

March 19

On Hearing a Symphony of Beethoven

"Sweet sounds, oh, beautiful music, do not cease!
Reject me not into the world again.
With you alone is excellence and peace,
Mankind made plausible, his purpose plain.
Enchanted in your air benign and shrewd,
With limbs a-sprawl and empty faces pale,
The spiteful and the stingy and the rude,
Sleep like the scullions in the fairy-tale.
This moment is the best the world can give:
The tranquil blossom on the tortured stem.
Reject me not, sweet sounds! Oh, let me live,
Till Doom espy my towers and scatter them,
A city spell-bound under the aging sun,
Music my rampart, and my only one."

Edna St. Vincent Millay
American Poet (1892-1950)

March 20

"...the words uttered by Beethoven on his deathbed:
'I believe I am as yet but at the beginning.'"

Ludwig van Beethoven

March 21

Birthday of Johann Sebastian Bach (1685-1750)
"Johann Sebastian Bach was born on March 21, 1685 in Eisenach, Germany. In the winter of 1705-1706, the young J.S. Bach made his legendary pilgrimage from Thuringia to Lubeck, walking nearly 260 miles each way, just to hear the celebrated artist, Dietrich Buxtehude, play an organ recital. What is most remarkable is that young Bach wrote down the entire organ recital by memory upon his return home."

Jan Chiapusso
Dutch/American Pianist and Teacher (1890-1969)
Author of "Bach's World"

March 22

"Music held an essentially spiritual meaning for Bach; it was a medium for reaching the depths of the soul...During Bach's school years, music was treated as one of the most important faculties within education. Luther had attributed a semi-magical quality to music, the power to convey ideas, to steer the will, to fortify faith. This evaluation of music can be traced back to Pythagoras and Plato, who considered musical training, 'a more potent instrument than any other, because rhythm and harmony (melody, in the ancient sense) find their way into the inward places of the soul'...The art of music was not the work of man, but a 'most wonderful and glorious gift of God, which had the power to drive out Satan and to resist temptations and evil thoughts.'"

Jan Chiapusso

March 23

"'I give, after theology, music the nearest locum and highest honor,' Luther wrote of his school curriculum. The word locum in medieval school language is equivalent to a division in the plan of learning, but Luther used the term in its ancient sense of place, or classroom. The far-reaching influence of this conception upon the subsequent development and the idealistic character of German music can hardly be underestimated. Without this vision of music as a spiritual power the world would never have known the genius of Bach and Beethoven."

Jan Chiapusso

March 24

"...In Carolingian days, music was regarded as the most important 'discipline' in the school curriculum but even earlier, in the seventh century, Isidore of Seville had said, 'Nothing exists without her; for the world herself is composed of the harmony of sounds, and the Heaven moves itself according to the course of harmony,' an observation obviously based on Pythagorean conception that music is a part of the cosmic harmonia or proportion. Alcuin, Charlemagne's secretary and educational adviser, placed music among 'the seven columns which carry the divine wisdom,' and warned that 'no one could reach comprehensive knowledge who does not elevate himself by means of these seven pillars or steps.'"

Jan Chiapusso

March 25

" ...The elaborate coloratura passages of the cantatas and motets designated for performance each week demanded a skill in sight singing that is rarely found today, except among a few highly trained professionals. It certainly would be impossible today to gather a group of choir boys ranging in age from 11 to 23 who could meet the exacting requirements of the music and master like Johann Sebastian Bach. Only an unshaken faith in the spiritual purpose of the art and a long tradition of adherence to rigid disciplines could produce such a concerted musical dedication on the part of composers, teachers, and students."

Jan Chiapusso

March 26

"Music theory, as taught in the Gymnasia, was focused primarily on achievement of the highly developed technique of sight-singing called solfeggio . . . Before Luther's time, musical instruction at the universities was treated as a scientia or a doctrina, closely allied to mathematics, as part of the quadrivium. The Lutheran schools followed this approach to some extent, but did not sacrifice teaching musical performance. Gradually, the venerable classics of the Middle Ages, Pythagoras, and Boethius, were relegated to the classrooms of university lectures, where pure music sunk into oblivion."

Jan Chiapusso

March 27

"From the time Bach gave up writing for the church (1742-1750), he submitted himself to a rigorous discipline, and for a twofold reason: besides his desire to sharpen his acuteness in contrapuntal perception and quick insight into all possible moves of the intervals and their harmonic combinations, the metaphysics of Werckmeister, Kepler, and their Pythagorean mysticism had taught him that this very discipline dealt with fundamental, primary elements of the divine spirit. The infinite possibilities of intervallic combinations within the movement from dissonance to consonance was the creativity of the divine spirit. 'Anyone could do as well, if only he work as hard as I have,' he told his student."

Johann Sebastian Bach
Jan Chiapusso

March 28

"Figured bass is the most perfect foundation of music. It is executed with both hands in such a manner that the left hand plays the notes that are written, while the right adds consonances and dissonances thereto, making an agreeable harmony for the glory of God and the justifiable gratification of the soul. Like all music, the figured bass should have no other end and aim than the glory of God and the recreation of the soul; where this is not kept in mind, there is no true music, but only an infernal clamour and ranting."

Johann Sebastian Bach
German Composer, Organist and Church Musician (1685-1750)

March 29

"Do not judge a composition on a first hearing; that which pleases most at first is not always the best. Masters call for study. Many things will only become clear to you when you are old."

Robert Schumann

March 30

"Music is the latest of the arts to have developed, her beginnings were the simple moods of joy and sorrow (major and minor). Indeed, the less cultivated man can scarcely believe that there exist more specialized emotions, whence his difficulty in understanding the more individual masters such as Beethoven and Schubert. We have learned to express the more delicate nuances of feeling by penetrating more deeply into the mysteries of harmony."

Robert Schumann

March 31

Birthday of Franz Joseph Haydn (1732-1809)
"...the musician constructs...with a view to the spiritual; the artist is on his true course when with the aid of sonorities, he shows the flight of constructive thought towards its origins from where beauty emanates."

Robert Schumann

April

Lake Pepin on the Mississippi River in Minnesota

April 1

Birthday of Sergei Rachmaninoff (1873-1943)
"Music is the imagination of love in sound.
It is what man imagines of his life, and his life is love."

W. J. Turner
Australian Writer (1889-1946)

April 2

"I think before we can understand the music of heaven, we will have to go beyond our earthly concept of music. I think most earthly music will seem to us to have been written in the 'minor key' in comparison to what we are going to hear in heaven. Angels have a celestial language and make music that is worthy of the God who made them. I believe in heaven, we will be taught the language and music of the celestial world. We believe that on earth, all mankind can be taught the language of music as an essential prelude to the joy of heaven's music."

Billy Graham

April 3

"In the middle of the Old Testament, we find the hymnbook that God inspired and that Jesus sang from in the Upper Room the night before His death (Matthew 26:30). The 150 psalms speak of praise well over 150 times. Our imagination cannot begin to fathom what it must have been like to see Jesus sitting with the disciples, singing hymns of praise, knowing that the very next day, He would die for the sins of the world. Many theologians believe that Jesus would have led the disciples in the Hallel psalms (praise hymns), which appear in various chapters of the Book of Psalms: 'In You, O Lord, I put my trust . . . You are my rock and my fortress . . . Lead me and guide me.'"

Billy Graham

April 4

"Nothing exists without music for the universe itself is said to have been framed by a kind of harmony of sounds and the Heaven itself revolves under the tones of that harmony."

Isidore of Seville
Spanish Archbishop (560-636)

April 5

"Our tradition teaches us that sound is God – 'Nada Brahma.' That is, musical sound and the musical experience are steps to the realization of the self. We view music as a kind of spiritual discipline that raises one's inner being to divine peacefulness and bliss. We are taught that one of the fundamental goals a Hindu works toward in his lifetime is a knowledge of the true meaning of the universe – its unchanging, eternal essence – and this is realized first by a complete knowledge of one's self and one's own nature. The highest aim of our music is to reveal the essence of the universe it reflects. The ragas are among the means by which this essence can be apprehended. Thus, through music, one can reach God."

Ravi Shankar
Indian Musician and Teacher (1920 - 2012)

April 6

"The armed eye beholds the stars; the unarmed only sees fog shadows."

Robert Schumann

April 7

"The destiny of music, like that of life, is an eternal ascendance . . . It would be a puny art, indeed, that merely possessed sounds and no speech nor signs to express the state of the soul."

Robert Schumann

April 8

Robert Schumann (1810-1856), pianist, composer, writer and highly imaginative artist wrote with great insight and eloquence about the artists and music of his time. In the music magazine, the *"Neue Zeitshrift fur Musik,"* (New Music Journal) of which Schumann was founder, he wrote most descriptively about the way in which Beethoven reflected on the beauty of nature, related these experiences to life and then translated these emotional portraits into music. "As soon as the first few of his works appeared, his fame was established forever . . . So rich an artistic life, many of his works, perhaps, best be compared to a splendidly landscaped garden with paths which wind to often wonderful effect among woodland, meadows, valleys, and rocky gorges. As in gardens of that nature one comes, generally surprisingly, upon the most breathtaking views, which are often fully appreciated only by the experienced eye, so in a magnificent artist garden, such as that which Herr. v. B. has created for us, certain enthralling features are particularly evident. Here, as there, the paths sometimes so suddenly change directions, and often just as one is at the most enchanting and restful spots, that one thinks, at least during the first moments, one is going back or that one has turned off from the route on which one has hoped for still more beautiful artistic pleasures, the loss of which one now regrets. However, both there and here, one should allow oneself, willingly and submissively, to be guided by the creator of the work of art - Herr v. B."

Robert Schumann

April 9

"It is the artist's lofty mission to shed light
into the very depths of the human heart."

Robert Schumann

April 10

"As a conductor, our Master (Beethoven) could in no wise, be called a model, and the orchestra had to pay heed lest it be misled by its mentor, for he thought only of his tone poems, and was carelessly engaged in calling attention to their authentic expression by means of the most manifold gesticulations. Thus he often struck down with his baton at a strong dynamic point, though it might occur on the weak beat of the measure. He was accustomed to indication of a diminuendo by trying to make himself physically smaller and smaller, and at the pianissimo, slipped under the conductor's desk, so to say. As the tonal masses increased in volume, he, too, seemed to swell, as though out of a contraction, and with the entrance of the entire body of instrumental tone, he rose on the tips of his toes, grew to well-nigh giant size, and swaying in the air with his arms, seemed to be trying to float up into the clouds. He was all active movement, no organic part of himself as idles, and the whole man might be compared to a perpetual mobile."

Ignaz von Seyfried
Austrian Musician, Conductor and Composer (1776-1841)

April 11

"Beethoven was very meticulous with regard to expression, the more delicate shadings, an equalized distribution of light and shade, and an effective tempo rubato, and without betraying the slightest impatience always took pleasure in discussing them individually with the various musicians. And then, when he saw that the musicians had grasped his ideas, and moved, carried away and filled with enthusiasm by the magic charm on his tonal creations, were playing together with increasing fervor, his face would be illumined with joy, all his features would radiate happiness and content, a satisfied smile would wreathe his lips, and a thundering "Bravi tutti" would reward the successful artistic achievement."

Ignaz von Seyfried

April 12

"The great masters stimulate and refresh the awareness of the spirit. As everyone knows, there are no depths of unhappiness, tragedy, frustration, anger, and despair, that haven't touched Mozart, for instance, to the very core of his being; nor was there any nuance, any form of delight that passed him by. An inspired musician will wed his life to the essence of the piece, demonstrating the glow, the swiftly-changing visions through the symbols that were Mozart's language. Some of our young pianists don't seem to let all this shine through the notes of the score. It was Goethe who said that we go through periods of history which are stamped either by spirit or the signs of technical progress. But the times which will be remembered are the epochs of spiritual enlightenment, lifting mankind

Godward – not the technical achievements, even if they should be beneficial and spectacular. It would do our youngsters good to have these thoughts instilled in them."

Lili Kraus

April 13

"...the orchestra...has to be transcended to convey the essence of the music; and so, the piano must also be transcended to produce a sound that is the sound of all sounds. Behind the sounds and through them, the composer is able to relate his cosmic experience."

Lili Kraus

April 14

The lyrics of the hymn arrangement of Beethoven's "Ode to Joy" that is both beautifully suited to the melody and spirit of Beethoven, were written by Henry Jackson van Dyke in 1907 while staying at the home of a friend at Williams College, Massachusetts. Van Dyke was born on November 10, 1852 in Germantown, Pennsylvania, attended Princeton University, served as pastor of the Brick Presbyterian Church in New York City and later returned to Princeton as a professor of English literature. He chaired a committee that, in 1905, compiled the *Presbyterian Book of Common Worship* with his hymn arrangement of "Ode to Joy" first appearing in the Presbyterian Hymnal in 1911. Some of Van Dyke's quotes that have been widely published give a glimpse into the spirit and wisdom of the man: "There is a loftier ambition than merely to stand high in the world. It is to stoop down and lift mankind a little higher."

Henry Jackson van Dyke
Pastor and Writer (1852-1933)

April 15

"Use the talents you possess, for the woods would be very silent
if no birds sang except the best."

Henry Jackson van Dyke

April 16

Van Dyke coupled his lyrics with the musical arrangement of "Ode to Joy" composed by Edward Hughes in 1824. Based on the scripture from Psalm 71:23, *"Joyful, Joyful, We Adore Thee"* is in the public domain and remains a great resource for all who love and teach Beethoven's "Ode to Joy."

Joyful, Joyful, We Adore Thee

"Joyful, joyful, we adore Thee, God of glory, Lord of love;
Hearts unfold like flowers before Thee, opening to the sun above.
Melt the clouds of sin and sadness; drive the dark of doubt away;
Giver of immortal gladness, fill us with the light of day!

All Thy works with joy surround Thee,
Earth and heaven reflect Thy rays,
Stars and angels sing around Thee, center of unbroken praise.
Field and forest, vale and mountain, flowery meadow, flashing sea,
Singing bird and flowing fountain call us to rejoice in Thee.

Thou art giving and forgiving, ever blessing, ever blessed,
Wellspring of the joy of living, ocean depth of happy rest!
Thou our Father, Christ our Brother, all who live in love are Thine;
Teach us how to love each other, lift us to the joy divine.

Mortals, join the happy chorus, which the morning stars began;
Father love is reigning o'er us, brother love binds man to man.
Ever singing, march we onward, victors in the midst of strife,
Joyful music leads us Sunward in the triumph song of life."

Henry Jackson van Dyke

April 17

"Time is too slow for those who wait, too swift for those who fear, too long for those who grieve, too short for those who rejoice, but for those who love, time is eternity."

"Who seeks for Heaven alone to save his soul,
May keep the path, but will not reach the goal;
While he who walks in love may wander far,
Yet God will bring him where the blessed are."

Henry Jackson van Dyke

April 18

"Music comes eons before religion..."

Alfred North Whitehead
English Mathematician and Philosopher (1861-1947)

April 19

"Music is not illusion, but revelation rather. Its triumphant power resides in the fact that it reveals to us beauties we find nowhere else, and that the apprehension of them is not transitory, but a perpetual reconcilement to life."

Peter Ilich Tchaikovsky
Russian Composer (1840-1893)

April 20

"You ask whether I had a particular program in mind when I composed this symphony. I generally reply to questions of this sort about my symphonic works: nothing of the sort. Actually it is extremely difficult to answer this question. How can one interpret those vague feelings which course through one during the composition of an instrumental work, without reference to a definite subject? It is a purely lyrical process. A sort of confession of the soul in music; an accumulation of material flowing forth again in notes just as the lyric poet pours himself out expression and is a more subtle medium for translating the thousand shifting moments of the feelings of the soul."

Peter Ilich Tchaikovsky

April 21

"...music does not reside in the notes, but between them."

Gustav Mahler
Austrian Composer (1860-1911)

April 22

"If one wishes to make music, one should not paint or write poetry or desire to describe anything. But what one makes music out of is still the whole - that is the feeling, thinking, breathing, suffering human being. There would be no objection of a 'program,' though this may not be exactly the highest step on the ladder, provided that it is a musician who is expressing himself in it and not a writer, philosopher, or painter, all of these being contained in the musician."

Gustav Mahler

April 23

"It is the peculiarity of Beethoven's imagination that again and again he lifts us to a height from which we re-evaluate not only all music but all life, all emotion, and all thought. This peculiarity has long been recognized as the function of the greatest literature."

Ernest Newman
English Music Critic and Musicologist (1868-1959)

April 24

Speaking to George Nageli in 1824, Beethoven said: "The description of a picture belongs to the field of painting; in this the poet can count himself more fortunate than my muse for his territory is not so restricted as mine in this respect, though mine, on the other hand, extends into other regions. My dominion is not easily reached."

Ludwig van Beethoven

April 25

"Music is the only bodiless entry into a higher world of knowledge which comprehends mankind but is not comprehended by it."

Ludwig van Beethoven

April 26

"Jesus looked at them and said,
'With man this is impossible, but not with God;
all things are possible with God.'"

Mark 10:27
The Bible

April 27

"Therefore we do not lose heart. Though outwardly we are wasting away, yet inwardly we are being renewed day by day. For our light and momentary troubles are achieving for us an eternal glory that far outweighs them all. So we fix our eyes not on what is seen, but on what is unseen. For what is seen is temporary, but what is unseen is eternal."
2 Corinthians 4:16-18

The Bible

April 28

"It's very unfortunate, young folks today are imitating rather than creating music themselves. They tell each other 'Horowitz plays this way, Rubinstein plays that way, Arrau plays another way; I like this one best, I play like this.' It's as if they are going to a market. Music is not like that; music is based on individualism."

Vladimir Horowitz

April 29

"Bach is my best friend. Bach is forever, and nobody, nobody will reach the greatness and profoundness and the diversity of Bach. He is the God of music, the image of what I dream in music and what I say in music."

Pablo Casals

April 30

"In every style, in every feeling, Bach is exuberant! When I played the Suites for the Cello alone for the first time in Germany, the purists said that this was not Bach and the others said that it was a real discovery. Now the Bach at that time was played like an exercise without any real musical meaning. They were afraid to put something in it. They were afraid and even now many of the artists of today have accepted the bad theory that the music of Bach is objective. And it is the contrary, absolutely the contrary! It is the most free, the more poetic, the more everything. I advise the young musician not to fear Bach. Everything, every feeling, everything lovely, tragic, dramatic, poetic, everything, every feeling most profound – is Bach. Bach never says a useless thing but something always so important. Yes, Bach is universal and has said in music everything that we desire in life. This is Bach: the greatest fantasy, the greatest liberty."

Pablo Casals

May

Cook Forest State Park in Cooksburg, Pennsylvania

May 1

"Be full of Joy. Joy saves. Joy cures. Joy in Me.
In every ray of sunlight, every smile, every act of kindness, or love,
every trifling service - joy."

A. J. Russell

May 2

"The helping hand is needed that raises the helpless to courage, to struggle, to faith, to health. Love and laugh. Love and laughter are the beckoners to faith and courage and success. Trust on, love on, joy on."

A. J. Russell

May 3

"Seek in every way to become child-like. Seek, seek, seek until you find, until the years have added to your nature that of the trusting child. Not only for its simple trust must you copy the child-spirit, but for its joy in life, its ready laughter, its lack of criticism, its desire to share all with all men. Ask much that you may become as little children, friendly and loving towards all - not critical, not fearful. 'Except ye . . . become as little children, ye shall not enter into the kingdom of heaven.'"

A. J. Russell

May 4

"According to Franz Liszt . . . emphasis on self-teaching is the proper goal for any master to develop with his pupil; in his teaching, Liszt insisted 'First music, then studies' and the importance of a performing artist as not isolating himself from people and the world outside his own musical experience; Liszt further divined that 'all our playing is but the reflection of what we are.'"

Paul Roes

May 5

"The secret of life is enjoying the passage of time . . . The thing about time is that time isn't really real . . . The secret of love is in opening up your heart . . . 'Cause anyone knows that love is the only road."

James Taylor
American Singer-Songwriter (b.1948)

May 6

"What a strange paradox . . . Those (Franz Liszt) who are a light for so many others are doomed to solitude."

Paul Roes

May 7

Birthday of Johannes Brahms 1833-1897)
Birthday of Peter Ilich Tchaikovsky (1840-1893)
"If unfortunately, acquired knowledge has made him, the teacher, forget his first enthusiasm, the master can no longer effectively guide his young friend."

Paul Roes

May 8

"Only Divine Love grants the keys to science."

from A Season of Hell, 1914.
J. Arthur Rimbaud
French Poet (1854-1891)

May 9

"What love is to man, music is to the arts and mankind. Music is love itself - it is the purest, most ethereal language of passion, showing in a thousand ways all possible changes of color and feelings; and though only true in a single instance, it can be understood by thousands of men - who all feel differently."

Carl Maria von Weber
German Composer (1786-1826)

May 10

"You must bring the spiritual, emotional, technical, and intellectual aspects of music together, combined into one. Nothing should stick out. Intellect and mind is only control, not the guide. The guide is the control of emotion. The first point of music is emotion."

Vladimir Horowitz

May 11

"Scriabin once heard me play and he told my parents, 'Your son will be a great pianist. But most important, make of him a cultured man who knows about every aspect of art; not only piano, but composition, the aesthetics of music, the opera.'"

Vladimir Horowitz

May 12

"Cliff Barrows directed our music and his wife, Billie, played the piano in the early days of our crusades. Their ministry among the team was marked by joy - how appropriate, since joy often accompanies music. The Old Testament is filled with music, and King David was, perhaps, the very first music director, who appointed singers 'by raising the voice with resounding joy' (1 Chronicles 15:16)."

Billy Graham

May 13

"The Bible compares us to salt, lamps, yeast, and seed - none of which is of any use as long as it's kept in a closed container. Doing so might preserve them - but that isn't their purpose. Salt was meant to be sprinkled on food to preserve it or make it appetizing; lamps were meant to shine, dispelling the darkness and lighting our way; yeast was meant to leaven the flour so it can be baked and eaten; seed was meant to be sown so crops will grow and bear fruit . . . So too with us. How can we remain silent and unconcerned, bottling up the Gospel instead of sharing it with others? To do so is to miss God's purpose in keeping us here. Jesus said, 'You are the light of the world. A city on a hill cannot be hidden. Neither do people light a lamp and put it under a bowl. Instead they put it on it's stand, and it gives light to everyone in the house.'" (Matthew 5:14-15)

Billy Graham

May 14

"Music demands an alert mind of intellectual capacity, but it is far from being an intellectual exercise. Musical cerebration as a game for its own sake may fascinate a small minority of experts or specialists, but it has no true significance unless its rhythmic patterns and melodic designs, its harmonic tensions and expressive timbres penetrate the deepest layer of our subconscious mind."

Aaron Copland
American Composer (1900-1990)

May 15

"I have been concerned with the creation of music or more than thirty years, with no lessening of my sense of humility before the majesty of music's expressive power, before its capacity to make manifest a deeply spiritual resource of mankind."

Aaron Copland

May 16

"Therefore, the superior man tries to create harmony in the human heart by a rediscovery of human nature, and tries to promote music as a means to the perfection of human culture. When such music prevails and the people's minds are led toward the right ideals and aspirations, we may see the appearance of a great nation."

Confucius

May 17

"Music, like every art, is founded upon spiritual beauty, every creation of beauty bringing a new degree of spiritual perfection."

Ludwig van Beethoven

May 18

"Competitions are for horses, not artists."

Bela Bartok
Hungarian Composer and Pianist (1881-1945)

May 19

"I AM MUSIC, most ancient of the arts. I am more than ancient; I am eternal. Even before life commenced upon this earth, I was here in the winds and the waves. When the first trees and flowers and grasses appeared, I was among them. And when Man came, I at once became the most delicate, most subtle, and the most powerful medium for the expression of Man's emotions. When men were little better than beasts, I influenced them for their good.

In all ages, I have inspired men with hope, kindled their love, given a voice to their joys, cheered them on to valorous deeds, and soothed them in times of despair. I have played a great part in the drama of Life, whose end and purpose is the complete perfection of man's nature. Through my influence, human nature has been uplifted, sweetened and refined. With the aid of men, I have become a Fine Art. From Tubalcain to Thomas Edison, a long line of the brightest minds have devoted themselves to the perfection of instruments through which men may utilize my powers and enjoy my charms. I have myriads of voices and instruments.

I am in the hearts of all men and on their tongues, in all lands and among all peoples; the ignorant and unlettered know me, not less than the rich and learned. For I speak to all men, in a language that all understand. Even the deaf hear me, if they but listen to the voices of their own souls.

I am the food of love. I have taught men gentleness and peace; and I have led them onward to heroic deeds. I comfort the lonely, and I harmonize the discord of crowds. I am a necessary luxury to all men. I AM MUSIC."

Allan C. Inman
American Poet (1887-1975)

May 20

"Earth's troubles and difficulties will seem, even now, less overwhelming
as you look, not at the things that are seen
but at the real, the Eternal Life."

James Van Praagh
American Psychic and Author (1958-)
Author of "Talking to Heaven"

May 21

"Even though it might not be clear right now, your light on this earth is needed. There is no one else on earth like you because you are indeed unique. People need you! Tell yourself how much you love and appreciate yourself for being alive and having the strength and courage to go through such an incredible adventure called life!"

James Van Praagh

May 22

Birthday of Richard Wagner (1813-1883)
The famous architect Frank Lloyd Wright designed many beautiful buildings, homes and other magnificent structures. Toward the end of his career, a reporter asked him, "Of your many beautiful designs, which one is your favorite?" Without missing a beat, Frank Lloyd Wright answered, "My next one."

Frank Lloyd Wright
American Architect (1867-1959)

May 23

"...the view of art as spirit-born never lost exponents. Goethe, Hegel, and Schopenhauer all speak of art in relationship to divine wisdom and to the Ideal. Schopenhauer, along with many other great thinkers, felt that music occupies a special position among the arts. He thought music to be the direct expression of the Divine in nature..."

Arthur Schopenhauer
German Philosopher (1788-1860)

May 24

"The unutterable depth of all music by virtue of which it floats through our consciousness as the vision of a paradise firmly believed in yet ever distant from us, and by which also it is so fully understood and yet so inexplicable, rests on the fact that is restores to us all the emotions of our inmost nature, but entirely without reality and far removed from their pain."

Arthur Schopenhauer

May 25

"Music is the answer to the mystery of life. It is the most profound of all the arts. It expresses the deepest thoughts of life and being in simple language which nonetheless cannot be translated."

Arthur Schopenhauer

May 26

"The expression of joy as the final residuum of any meaningful experience conceived in creative terms is, however, common to all phases of Beethoven's work. Only the very great can convince us of the aesthetic validity of 'happy endings,' because only through the demonstration of their capacity to suffer everything without being broken convince us that they have earned that right . . . The high-treble trills at the termination of Beethoven's last piano sonata C minor, opus 111, ascending into some Nirvana stratosphere of white light beyond the imaginings of birds or astronauts, complement perfectly the volcanic opening movement, Beethoven's farewell to rebelliousness which he this time labeled 'Appassionata' (Piano Sonata opus 57) on his own. But the ending of Beethoven's Symphony No. 9, opus 125, is the happiest of all."

Selden Rodman
American Writer (1909-2002)
Author of "The Heart of Beethoven"

May 27

"All imitation is as nothing compared with originality."

Frederic Chopin

May 28

"Chopin was the master poet of the pedal. He was most particular in teaching it and reiterated frequently: 'The correct employment of it remains a study for life.'"

Paul Roes

May 29

"Beethoven was deaf, as you know. He suffered from kidney stones, which is a very painful condition. He had hepatitis; he had multiple episodes of gastrointestinal infections. For someone to have that many maladies and to suffer so greatly and yet produce superhuman music, music that can actually elevate the spirit to a much different plane that this ordinary plane we live in, is quite phenomenal."

Dr. Alfredo Che Guevara Jr.
American Surgeon (1951-)
Author of "Beethoven's Hair"

May 30

"There is no more fascinating personality in music history than Ludwig van Beethoven. With this spiritual giant, we have the true beginnings of modern pianism. The pianoforte became a means to an end in expressing the deepest emotions. Previous rules and traditions of piano technique meant nothing to him if they, in any way, hampered his inner feelings at the keyboard. Here is the first major pianist directly to oppose 'the finger school' and its harpsichord ancestry."

Reginald Gerig
Piano Professor, Author (1920-)
Author of "Famous Pianists and Their Technique"

May 31

"The message is what matters. It was no caprice that Beethoven admired above all his predecessors a composer who took the same view. 'My lord,' Handel once reproved a patron who had complimented him on the 'noble entertainment' offered by '*The Messiah*,' 'I should be sorry if I only entertained them. I wish to make them better!'"

Selden Rodman

June

Our Beethoven Sand Art at Daytona Beach Shores, Florida

June 1

In Selden Rodman's book, *"The Heart of Beethoven,"* the author wrote, "Beethoven had had a poem of Schiller in mind for some such dimly foreseen eventuality ever since he grew up in Bonn. Sketches of the setting date from 1794, 1798, 1811 and 1822 . . . Its key line 'All mankind shall be as brothers' summed up succinctly Beethoven's ideal of social destiny . . . The chorale rises to its most dizzying heights as human brotherhood expands to cover the universe: 'Seek Him beyond the canopy of Heaven! He must dwell above the stars.'" During the composition of Symphony No. 9, in a letter to Archduke Rudolph dated July 1, 1823, Beethoven wrote, "I thank Him who is above the stars, that I am beginning to use my eyes again."

Ludwig van Beethoven

June 2
Birthday of Sir Edward Elgar (1857-1834)

Friedrich Schiller's poetry from the final movement of
Beethoven's Symphony No. 9 "Ode to Joy"

"O friends, not these strains -
Rather let us sing more pleasing songs, and more joyous.
(these introductory words added by Beethoven)
Joy, thou gleaming spark divine, Daughter of Elysium,
Drunk with ardor, we draw near, Goddess, to thy shrine.
Thy magic unites again what custom sternly drew apart;
All mankind become brothers beneath thy gentle hovering wing.
He whose happy fortune grants him friend to have and friend to be,
Who has won a noble woman, let him join in our rejoicing!
Yes - even were it one heart only beating for him in the world!
But if he's never known this, let him weeping steal from out our ranks.
Joy is drawn by every creature from the breast of Nature;
All men good and all men evil walk upon her rose-strewn path.
Kisses gave she and the ripe grape, a good friend, trusty to the last;
Even the worm can feel pleasure, and the Seraph stands before God.
Glad as suns that He hurtles through the vast spaces of heaven,
Pursue your pathway, brothers; be joyful as a hero in victory.
Millions, be you embraced! For the universe, the kiss!
Brothers - above the canopy of stars a loving Father surely dwells.
Millions, do you fall upon your knees? Do you sense the Creator, world!
Seek Him above the canopy of stars! Surely He dwells above the stars."

Ludwig van Beethoven
Friedrich Schiller
German Poet, Philosopher, Historian (1759-1805)

June 3
From an account of the premier of Beethoven's Symphony No. 9 – Part 1
The following story was told to Sir George Grove exactly as written by
Madame Sabatier-Ungher in the end gallery of the Crystal Palace Concert
Room during her visit to London in 1869: "At the actual first performance
of Beethoven's Symphony No. 9 on May 7, 1824, a great deal of emotion
was naturally enough visible in the orchestra; and we hear of such
eminent players as Mayseder and Bohm even weeping. At the close of
the performance an incident occurred which must have brought the tears
of many an eye in the room."

Ludwig van Beethoven
Sir George Grove
English Writer, Author "Grove's Dictionary of Music and Musicians"
(1820-1900)

June 4

Beethoven's Symphony No. 9 Premier - Part 2

"Beethoven, though placed in the midst of this confluence of music, heard nothing of it at all and was not even sensible of the applause of the audience at the end of his great work, but continued standing with his back to the audience, and beating the time, till Fraulein Ungher, who had sung the contralto part, turned him, or induced him to turn round and face the people, who were still clapping their hands, and giving way to the greatest demonstrations of pleasure."

Sir George Grove/Ludwig van Beethoven

June 5

Beethoven's Symphony No. 9 Premier - Part 3

"Beethoven's turning round and the sudden conviction thereby forced on everybody that he had not done so before because he could not hear what was going on, acted like an electric shock on all present, and a volcanic explosion of sympathy and admiration followed, which was repeated again and again and seemed as if it would never end."

Sir George Grove/Ludwig van Beethoven

June 6

In Martin Cooper's book, *"Beethoven: The Last Decade,"* the author wrote, "Under what influences, in exactly what labour of the imagination and the spirit that innocent introductory flourish (of the first movement of the 9th) swelled and burgeoned, like an acorn swelling into an oak tree, it is impossible to say; but it is hard to resist the feeling that the uniquely indeterminate yet pregnant atmosphere of the introductory bars has some extra-musical affinity. We may never know . . . the exact nature of that . . . extra-musical origin, but Beethoven himself gives us a warrant for divining its presence."

Ludwig van Beethoven
Martin Cooper
English Author (1910-1986)

June 7

The London German with whom Beethoven got on so famously in 1824, J. A. Stumpff, reported Beethoven as saying, "When I contemplate in wonderment the firmament and the host of luminous bodies which we call worlds and suns, eternally revolving within its boundaries, my spirit soars beyond these stars, many millions of miles away towards the fountain from which all created work springs and from which all new creation must still flow (and it is from there that I found the music for Symphony No. 9.")

Ludwig van Beethoven
Johann Andreas Stumpff
German Piano Maker (1769-1846)

June 8

Birthday of Robert Schumann (1810-1856)
"I feel strongly that the great fundamentals should be more discussed in all public meetings and also in meetings of schools and colleges, not only the students but also the faculty should get down to more thinking and action about the great problems which concern all countries and all people in the world today, and not let the politicians do it all and have the whole say."

Charles Ives
American Composer (1874-1954)

June 9

"I have often been told that it is not the function of music, or a concert, to concern itself with matters of the day. But I do not by any means agree. I think that it is one of the things that music can do, if it happens to want to, if it comes naturally, and is not the result of superimposition - I have had some fights about this.."

Charles Ives

June 10

There is such power in words. From the Scriptures, the Beatitudes of Jesus can be interpreted as *"Be Attitudes."* What "attitudes" do we choose to "be" and to have? When there is "evil" in the world, it's as though people get turned around in life with evil being the word "live" spelled backwards. When we contemplate the stars, we can consider the "universe," as a universal opportunity for all of us to share in "one verse." (uni-verse)

Don and Delayna Beattie
Music Educators

June 11

"We don't see things as they are, we see them as we are."

Anais Nin
Cuban-French Author (1903-1977)

June 12

"Everything became for Liszt a more and more intense concentration, an internal enchantment. He had understood that existence has no meaning until one knows how to forget self. Thus he loved life, which he felt within himself, that he perceived in his fellow man, and in everything. He understood that only he who loves can admire."

Paul Roes

June 13

"Liszt was not at all a man like others. One always felt that his suggestions came from a mystical thought. He saw further than we did, and when he spoke, his thoughts were so well considered that he gave the impression of seeing with eyes of a creator..."

Paul Roes

June 14

"Mozart speaks the mysterious language of a distant spiritual kingdom, whose marvelous accents echo in our inner being and arouse a higher intensive life."

E.T.A. Hoffmann
German Romantic Author (1776-1822)

June 15

"Sensitivity to harmonic change is an extremely important fact in creating a musically satisfying performance. At moments of heightened intensity resulting from an unexpected or particularly expressive harmonic progression, the performer must understand the idea from the 'theoretical' viewpoint and also be able to convey the 'emotional' content to the listeners. There should not be knowledge without 'feeling' nor 'feeling' without knowledge. The student who knows the names of chords and can identify 'intellectually' with what is happening must still learn to use such knowledge to illuminate the music. If he does not bridge the gap between theory and emotional content, the playing will sound dull and inexpressive. Conversely, the student who is all 'feeling' but does not coordinate his expression with the appropriate harmonic or melodic occurrence in the music in the music, will make it sound disjointed and even tasteless. For really gratifying playing, both elements, knowledge and feeling, must be brought into a direct relationship to each other."

Martin Canin
Julliard Piano Professor (1930-)

June 16

"They say that Beethoven's performance was not so much 'playing' as 'painting with tones,' while others express it as recalling the effect of 'reciting' all of which are attempts to state the fact that in his playing, the means - the passages, the execution, technical appliances - disappeared before the transcendent effect and meaning of the music . . . He was not particular in polishing and refining his performance, as were Hummel, Wolffl, Kalkbrenner, and others: indeed, such 'special' artists he satirically calls 'gymnasts' and expresses the opinion that 'the increasing mechanism of pianoforte playing would in the end, destroy all truth of expression in music.'"

Ludwig van Beethoven
Ernst Pauer
Austrian Pianist (1826-1905)

June 17

Birthday of Igor Stravinsky (1882-1971)
"Musical imagery is a concrete reality, not a metaphysical idea. The motivation of chords, phrasing, dissonances, rhythmic patterns, types of touch, dynamic, and accents are among the many images that should be clearly heard by our 'mind's ear.' Music structures higher emotions. It transforms lower emotions into higher emotions, and in this way, the feelings and the heart are cultured and awareness is raised to universal awareness. From the abstract influence of musical imagery comes concrete evolution on the most refined levels of life."

Maharishi Mahesh Yogi
Spiritual Teacher (1918-2008)
from "The Science of Creative Intelligence"

June 18

"Our study is in three basic areas: first, we consider the basic materials of music – harmony, melody, form, rhythm, and imagery – their range of influence, their evolution, and their structure. Second, we deal with the human element in music. This involves examining the role of the development of consciousness, discipline, skill in action, refinement or perception; and the creative and recreative processes of the composer, performer, and listener. Third, we examine the results of the musician's having breathed life into the musical materials..."

Maharishi Mahesh Yogi

June 19

"O! Music, echo of another world, manifestation of a Divine being within ourselves, when speech is impotent and our hearts are numb, Yours alone is the voice with which men cry out to one another from the depths of their prison, You it is who end their desolation, in whom are resolved the only outpourings of their grief."

Jean Paul Richter
German Writer (1763-1825)

June 20

"In recognizing the existence of a master rhythm in the universe, in seeing that each thing around us, in us, and done by us, has a rhythm, in admitting also that the artist, a being sensitive to these phenomena, feels he lives in the middle of rhythms and currents, we have only accomplished the first stage of the journey that leads to the comprehension of a musical work."

Paul Roes

June 21

"Know that one of the privileges given a possessor of great wealth (a wise teacher), is to watch others in the midst of their own joy of discovery, knowing that they, too, can be rewarded with the same riches."

Paul Roes

June 22

"There exists a secret bond between kindred spirits in every period. You who belong together, close your ranks ever more tightly, that the Truth of Art may shine more clearly, diffusing joy and blessings over all things."

Robert Schumann

June 23

"Musicke doth withdraw our minds from earthly cogitations,
lifteth up our spirits into heaven, maketh them light and celestial."

St. John Chrysostom
Archbishop of Constantinople (345-407)

June 24

"Your brain can store 100 trillion facts. Your mind can handle 15,000 decisions a second, as is the case when your digestive system is working. Your nose can smell up to 10,000 different odors. Your touch can detect an item 1/25,000th of an inch thick, and your tongue can taste one part of quinine in 2 million parts of water. You are a bundle of incredible abilities, an amazing creation of God."

Rick Warren
American Minister and Author (1954-)
from "The Purpose Driven Life"

June 25

"The supreme harmony of the Cosmos is reflected in the harmony of the spirit. It would greatly benefit those who study music seriously, if they were introduced into this domain, but the manual work preoccupies them so much that they forget to rise again to the source."

Franz Liszt

June 26

"The dominant factor in almost all of Liszt's compositions is his continuous rising above self . . . Contrary to other composers, Liszt did not describe his own feelings. He guided us toward heights from which one contemplates the wide spaces that stretch out around our lives."

Paul Roes

June 27

"If music is of all the arts the most readily accessible,
the reason is that it is cosmic rather than cosmopolitan."

Ignace Paderewski
Polish Concert Pianist (1860-1941)

June 28

"Let your light so shine before men, that they may see your good works and glorify your Father in heaven."

Matthew 5:16
The Bible

June 29

The experience of hearing Beethoven improvise was not easily forgotten. The effect was still a vivid memory when Carl Czerny wrote the following description in 1852, a quarter of a century after Beethoven's death: "His improvisation was most brilliant and striking. In whatever company he might chance to be, he knew how to produce such an effect upon every hearer that frequently not an eye remained dry, while many would break out into loud sobs; for there was something wonderful in his expression in addition to the beauty and originality of his ideas and his spirited style of rendering them. . . No one equaled Beethoven in rapidity of scales, double trills, skips - when playing, his demeanor was masterfully quiet, noble and beautiful, without the slightest grimace. Beethoven's performance of slow and sustained passages produced an almost magical effect upon every listener and, so far as I know, was never surpassed." Czerny also realized that both Beethoven's playing and his compositions were far ahead of his time.

Carl Czerny
Austrian Composer, Teacher, Pianist (1791-1857)

June 30

"Without music, life would be a mistake."
Freidrich Wilhelm Nietzsche
German Philosopher (1844-1900)

July

Elk in Downtown Estes Park, Colorado

July 1

"Without music the state cannot exist. All the disorders, all the wars we behold throughout the world occur only because of the neglect to learn music. Does not war result from the lack of unison among men? Thus, were all men to learn music, would not this be the means of agreement between them and of seeing universal peace reign all over the world?"

Jean-Baptiste Poquelin Moliere
French Playwright and Actor (1622-1673)

July 2

"All that ascends converges."

Reverend Father Pierre Teilhard de Chardin
French Philosopher and Jesuit Priest (1881-1955)

July 3

"You are not a human being in search of a spiritual experience.
You are a spiritual being immersed in a human experience."

Pierre Teilhard de Chardin

July 4

"In the end, it's not the years in your life that count.
It's the life in your years."

President Abraham Lincoln
(1809-1865)

"I like the dreams of the future better than the history of the past . . .
Don't talk about what you have done or what you are going to do . . .
Peace and friendship with all mankind is our wisest policy. I wish we may
be permitted to pursue it."

President Thomas Jefferson
(1743-1826)

"Observe good faith and justice toward all nations.
Cultivate peace and harmony with all."

President George Washington
(1732-1799)

July 5

Please Grant My Wish for Peace

"Dear God created all, entrusted to our care,
When something's done to make things better, May I be there.
Dear God we're out of hand, there's war upon our land,
If You bring peace unto the world, May I be there.
Giving to others is what we must do,
Friends in all nations, we're singing for you,
If I could change the world, the missiles would not fly,
All people hand in hand, Dear God,
Please grant my wish for peace.
To be a child of God, a peacemaker by trade,
So life is all the best it might be, Yes, I'll be there.
So enemies are friends, a house for everyone,
To help mankind love more and more, Yes, I'll be there.
Giving to others is what we must do,
Friends in all nations, we're singing for you,
If I could change the world, all the forests stand,

Kindness to all neighbors, Dear God,
Please grant my wish for peace.
Giving to others is what we must do,
Friends in all nations, we're singing for you,
If I could change the world, all the people sing,
All the people smiling, Dear God,
Please grant my wish for peace."

Donald Beattie
c. 1993 Edition HAS Music Publishing Co.

July 6

"Walking is the best possible exercise.
Habituate yourself to walk very far."

Thomas Jefferson

July 7

Birthday of Gustav Mahler (1860-1911)
"A symphony must be like the world. It must contain everything. . . Don't bother looking at the view - I have already composed it. . . If a composer could say what he had to say in words, he would not bother trying to say it in music."

Gustav Mahler

July 8

"Rest from your musical studies by industriously reading the poets.
Often take exercise out in the open."

Robert Schumann

July 9

"A man of learning and culture, Christian Gottlob Neefe, Beethoven's teacher, introduced Ludwig not only to the great musical classics, but the literary ones as well – Shakespeare, Goethe, Schiller, and the ancients of Greece and Rome. Neefe wrote, 'As a boy of eleven years old, Beethoven shows the most promising talent. He plays the clavier very skillfully and with power, reads at sight very well, and, to put it in a nutshell, he plays chiefly the *Well-Tempered Clavier* of Sebastian Bach. Whoever knows this collection of 48 Preludes and Fugues (which young Beethoven could transpose and play all of them in any key) will know what this means.' Years later, pianist Hans von Bulow would call Bach's 48 Preludes and Fugues the 'Old Testament' and Beethoven's 32 Piano Sonatas the 'New Testament' of keyboard literature."

Reginald Gerig
Christian Gottlob Neefe
German Composer, Conductor and Teacher (1748-1798)

July 10

In 1825, Beethoven said to his nephew, Karl, "I spend all my mornings with the muses, and they bless me also in my walks. On September 24, 1826, while in Gneixendorf, Beethoven told Gerhard von Breuning, "I never feel entirely well except when I am among scenes of unspoiled nature."

Ludwig van Beethoven

July 11

Louis Schlosser remarked that "In nature's open, Beethoven's creative powers drew their richest nourishment among the hills and the heavily leaved woods, and where ideas, as he expressed himself, flowed to him in quantity." Sir George Grove recorded a tradition that Beethoven refused to take possession of an engaged lodging because there were no trees near the house: "How is this? Where are your trees?" said Beethoven. "We have none," said the landlord. Beethoven replied, "Then the house won't do for me. I love a tree more than a man."

Louis Schlosser
German Violin Virtuoso and Composer (1800-1886)
Sir George Grove

July 12

To Mme. Streicher in 1817, Beethoven said "When you reach the old ruins, think that Beethoven often paused there; if you wander through the mysterious fir forests, think that I often poetized, or, as is said, composed there."

Ludwig van Beethoven

July 13

In 1818, Beethoven copied the following into his diary from Sturm's *"Essays on the World of God in Nature:"* "Nature is a glorious school for the heart! Tis well; I shall be a scholar in this school and bring an eager heart to her instruction. Here I shall learn wisdom . . . Here I shall learn to know God and find a foretaste of heaven in His knowledge. Among these occupations, my earthly days shall flow peacefully along until I am accepted into that world where I shall no longer be a student, but a knower of wisdom."

Ludwig van Beethoven

July 14

Ludwig van Beethoven's last country residence was in Gneixendorf, Austria, where he lived with his nephew Karl from September though December, 1826. His brother, Johann, owned the home where Beethoven lived as well as an estate nearby. While living in Gneixendorf, Beethoven composed the Opus 130 and 135 String Quartets. After Beethoven left Gneixendorf in the winter of 1826, his lodging, on the second floor of the home, remained nearly untouched until the Gettinger family purchased it in 1860. At the time the Beatties visited the residence in 1999, Maria Gettinger and her family maintained the home as a private residence. Upon Beethoven's return to Vienna from Gneixendorf, he took seriously ill and died on March 26, 1827.

In *"Beethoven: The Illustrated Lives of the Great Composers,"* Artes Orga wrote, "By the end of 1826, when Beethoven left Gneixendorf, he was a broken man, shabby, self-effacing, and racked with illness. For Beethoven, 1815-1827, were to be the years when his deafness became intolerable. He suffered, too, from rheumatism, catarrhal inflammation of the lungs, heart strain, jaundice (1821), a painful eye condition needing a darkened room and bandages (April 1823-January 1824), innumerable chills, nose-bleeding, appalling stomach disorders, ulcerative colitis, hepatitis, and in the end, dropsy, a terminal illness that took four months to run its course." The fact that Beethoven continued composing during these years of illness that included his Symphony No. 9, (1819-1823) as well as his profound late String Quartets, is nothing less than astonishing. In a word, Beethoven was a Titan."

Ludwig van Beethoven
Artes Orga
Producer and Writer (1944-)

July 15

"Music does not express the passions, love or longing of this or that situation. It is passion, love and longing."

Richard Wagner
German Opera Composer and Conductor (1813-1883)

July 16

"Over fifty times in the New Testament the phrase 'one another,' or 'each other' is used. We are commanded to love each other, pray for each other, encourage each other, admonish each other, greet each other, serve each other, teach each other, accept each other, honor each other, bear each other's burdens, forgive each other, submit to each other, be devoted to each other, and many other mutual tasks."

Rick Warren

July 17

Paul advised, "Live in harmony with each other. Don't try to act important, but enjoy the company of ordinary people. And don't think you know it all!" (Romans 12:16) To the Christians in Philippi he wrote, "Give more honor to others than to yourselves. Do not be interested only in your own life, but be interested in the lives of others." (Philippians 2:3-4)

Rick Warren

July 18

"Humility is not thinking less of yourself; it is thinking of yourself less. Humility is thinking more of others. Humble people are so focused on serving others, they don't think of themselves."

Rick Warren

July 19

"If all were determined to play the first violin, we should never have complete orchestras. Therefore, respect every musician in his proper field."

Robert Schumann

July 20

"Behind the mountains, there also dwell people. Be modest. You have never invented or discovered anything that others have not invented or discovered before. And even if you have, consider it as a gift from above which it is your duty to share with others."

Robert Schumann

July 21

"Seek out among your comrades those who know more than you do."

Robert Schumann

July 22

"Do not judge, and you will not be judged. Do not condemn, and you will not be condemned. Forgive, and you will be forgiven."

Luke 6:37
The Bible

July 23

"Our spiritual work is one of service and love. We must always aspire to bring as much love and understanding to everyone with whom we come in contact. Begin to live a life of love and service in all you encounter and all you do."

James Van Praagh

July 24

"Be a living example of the precept of love. See all things as an expression of that creative love called God. Know that there is no need for judgment, for judgment is of the lower physical self, or ego, and what right do you have to judge others because they haven't learned a certain human lesson yet? Judgment often stems from fear. Fear is not living in the God Self. Rather, fear prompts you to turn your back on the truth. Put away that which is not real; judgments, prejudices, and petty ego."

James Van Praagh

July 25

"Ardent as research may be, do not limit yourself to exploring exclusively the domain of the piano. The power of our means of execution depends also upon our general culture. 'All our playing is but the reflection of what we are.' (Liszt) True technique is nothing more than the manifestation of spiritual gifts. The lesson that Liszt has given to us is the most eloquent testimony of this."

Paul Roes

July 26

"Emotion is specific, individual, and conscious; music goes deeper than this, to the energies which animate our psychic life, and out of these creates a pattern which has an existence, laws, and human significance of it's own. It reproduces for us the most intimate essence, the tempo and the energy, of our spiritual being; our tranquility and our restlessness, our animation and our discouragement, our vitality and our weakness - all, in fact, of the fine shades of dynamic variation of our inner life. It reproduces these far more directly and more specifically than is possible through any other medium of human communication."

Roger Sessions
American Composer (1896-1985)

July 27

"Music is the divine way to tell beautiful, poetic things to the heart."

Pablo Casals

July 28

"Piano technique based on the simple natural laws penetrates the domain of music, a domain spiritual . . . It was the music which revealed to Liszt the secrets of the only natural piano technique suited for the piano."

Paul Roes

July 29

"For the piano, there is a single technique, which if complete, adapts itself as naturally to the work of Beethoven as to that of Mozart. I affirm, also, that all masterworks point the way to a single and unique technique. There is no separation of music from technique in any way. This separation between technique and music, so often commended, is the great misery of many musicians. This is what gives birth to those so-called techniques which should concern acrobats only. Great interpretation teaches us that all technique is included in the work itself."

Paul Roes

July 30

"Liberate yourself from all the exercises which preoccupy tens of thousands of pianists. Know that they are more harmful than useful."

Paul Roes

July 31

"And now I will show you the most excellent way. If I speak in the tongues of men and of angels, but have not love, I am only a resounding gong or a clanging cymbal. If I have the gift of prophecy and can fathom all mysteries and all knowledge, and if I have a faith that can move mountains, but have not love, I am nothing. . . Love is patient, love is kind, it does not envy, it does not boast, it is not proud. It is not rude, it is not self-seeking, it is not easily angered, it keeps no record of wrongs. Love does not delight in evil but rejoices with the truth. It always protects, always trusts, always hopes, always perseveres. Love never fails."

1 Corinthians 13:1-8

August

On the beach of Anguilla in the Eastern Caribbean

August 1

"Music is the arithmetic of the soul that does not know what it counts."

Gottfried Wilhelm Leibnitz
Philosopher and Mathematician (1646-1716)

August 2

"These measures (from Liszt's Sonata in B Minor) introduce a contemplation of transcendent inspiration that only rare humans can know. This reversed circle of reflection reveals Liszt's soul in all its' beauty. One can find this splendour in certain pages of the great mystics."

Paul Roes

August 3

"With Liszt, too, like Paganini, the attraction of space and the desire to detach himself from the world, were strong. He was conscious that solitude is no longer burdensome . . . It is from solitude that joy springs, the generous and peaceful conviction of power."

Paul Roes

August 4

"Only one who loves self can truly admire another."

Franz Liszt

August 5

"Understand, you can't give away what you don't have. If you don't love yourself, you're not going to be able to love others. If you're at strife on the inside, feeling angry or insecure about yourself, feeling unattractive, feeling condemned, then that's all you can give away. Please recognize that if you're negative toward yourself, it's not only affecting you. It is influencing every relationship you have and it will affect your relationship with God. That's why it's so important that you feel good about who you are. You may have some faults but lighten up. We all do. Interestingly, we might never outwardly criticize another yet we don't have any problem saying it to ourselves; thoughts like "you are really dumb, you're unattractive, you're undisciplined. If God approves you, why don't you start approving yourself?"

Joel Osteen

August 6

"Happiness is a decision you make, not an emotion you feel . . . The Bible says we are like a mist, a vapor; we're here for a moment, then we're gone. (James 4:14) Life is flying by, so don't waste another moment of your precious time being angry, unhappy, or worried. The psalmist said, 'This is the day which they Lord has made; let us rejoice and be glad in it.' (Psalm 118:24) Notice, he didn't say, 'Next week, when I don't have so many problems, I'm going to rejoice.' No, he said, 'This is the day.' This is the day that God wants you to choose to be happy."

Joel Osteen

August 7

"Happiness consists entirely in the imagination."

Wolfgang Amadeus Mozart

August 8

"The highest achievers in any field are those who do it because of passion, not duty or profit. We've all heard people say, 'I took a job I hate in order to make a lot of money, so someday I can quit and do what I love to do.' That's a big mistake. Don't waste your life in a job that doesn't express your heart. Remember, the greatest things in life are not things. Meaning is far more important than money. The richest man in the world once said, 'A simple life in the fear-of-God is better than a rich life with a ton of headaches.'" (Proverbs 15:16)

Rick Warren

August 9

"We must continually choose to keep our minds set on the higher things. The Bible says, 'Set your minds on the things which are above.' (Colossians 3:2) Notice again there is something that we are to do - we must continually choose, day in and day out, twenty-four hours a day, to keep our minds set on the higher things."

Joel Osteen

August 10

"Nothing can stop the man with the right mental attitude from achieving his goal. Nothing on earth can help the man with the wrong mental attitude."

Thomas Jefferson

August 11

"When you think about a problem over and over in your mind, that's called worry. When you think about God's Word (and the words of the great music masters) over and over in your mind, that's meditation. If you know how to worry, you already know how to meditate! You just need to switch your attention from your problems to Bible verses. The more you meditate on God's Word, the less you will have to worry about."

Rick Warren

August 12

"When I get up in the morning, I sit on the side of my bed and say, 'God, if I don't get anything else done today, I want to know You more and love you better.' God didn't just put me on earth just to fulfill a 'to-do list.' He's more interested in what I am than what I do. That's why we're called human beings, not human doings."

Rick Warren

August 13

"Remember, many of your first thoughts of the day
affect how you will live the rest of your day."

James Van Praagh

August 14

"...can we suppose that the philosopher constantly maintains in his daily
life the vision of the universe that comes to him in his moments
of finest insight?"

J.W.N. Sullivan

August 15

"Young Ferdinand Ries reported that at times, at 8:00 in the morning, after breakfast, Beethoven would say, 'Let us first take a short walk.' We went and frequently did not return until 3:00 or 4:00 that afternoon, having made a meal in some village. How much Beethoven's hearing had diminished was shown in 1802 during a walk in the country. His companion, Ferdinand Ries, called Beethoven's attention to a shepherd who played quite prettily in the woods upon a flute carved out of elderwood. For half an hour Beethoven could hear nothing. But notwithstanding, Ries assured Beethoven that he, too, heard nothing (which was not the case) and Beethoven sank into a melancholy mood. He grew monosyllabic, and stared straight before him with a gloomy look. On the way home, Beethoven kept on muttering to himself, all the time, humming and sometimes howling, always up and down, without singing any definite notes. There had occurred to him, he said, a theme for the last allegro of one of his piano sonatas. When he had entered his chamber with his companion, Beethoven ran with his hat on his head to the piano, and busied himself for almost an hour with the beautiful finale of the "Appassionata" Piano Sonata, opus 57. When he rose from the piano, he was surprised to see his young friend, Ries, still there, who had seated himself the meanwhile in a corner of the room. Beethoven said to him, "I can't give you a lesson today. I must still work."

Anton Schindler

August 16

"It would be a puny art, indeed, that merely possessed sounds and no speech nor signs to express the state of the soul . . . Music has been placed among those high mediums of art which have language and symbols for all spiritual states."

Robert Schumann

August 17

"Just so that genius exists it matters little how it appears, whether in the depths, as with Bach; on the heights, as with Mozart; or simultaneously in the depths and on the heights as with Beethoven." An inscription on an Opera House in Frankfort, Germany reads: "Bach gave us God's Word; Mozart gave us God's laughter; Beethoven gave us God's fire and God gave us prayer that we might pray without words."

Robert Schumann

August 18

"The function of the kind of music we have been discussing (Beethoven) is to communicate valuable spiritual states, and these states testify to the depth of the artist's nature and to the quality of his experience of life. Such states cannot usually be correlated with definite situations, and for that reason no program for them can be given. They are the fruits of countless experiences as realized and coordinated by the artist, and they enter into the very texture of his spiritual being."

J.W.N. Sullivan

August 19

"There has been demonstration of the universal truth by fugue, and it may be that more wisdom is to be found in that than in the religions and religious books of all the world together."

Sir Sacheverell Sitwell
English Writer (1897-1988)

August 20

"What the secrete working of Musick is in the myndes of men, as well appeareth hereby, that some of the ancient Philosophers, and those the moste wise, as Plato and Pythagoras, held for opinion, that the mind was made of a certaine harmonie and musical numbers, for the great compassion, and likeness of affection in the one and in the other, as also by that memorable history of Alexander: to whom when as Timotheus the great Musician played the Phrygian melody, it is said, that he was distraught with such unwonted fury, that, straightway rising from the table in great rage, he caused himself to be armed, as ready to go to warre, (for that musick is very warlike.) And immediately when as the Musician changed his stoke into the Lydian and Ionique harmony, he was so furr from warring, that he sat as style, as if he had been in matters of counsel. Such might is in musick: Wherefore Plato and Aristotle forbid the Acardian Melodie from children and youth. For that being altogether on the fyft and vii tone, it is of great force to molifie and quench the kindly courage, which useth to burne in yong brests. So that it is not incredible which the Poete here sayth, that Musick can breave the soule of sence."

Edmund Spenser
English Poet (1552-1599)
"The Secrete Working of Musick"

August 21

"...for even that vulgar and Tavern Musick, which makes one man merry another mad, strikes in me a deep fit of devotion, and a profound contemplation of the First Composer. There is something in it of Divinity more than the ear discovers: it is a Hieroglyphical and shadowed lesson of the Whole World, and creatures of God..."

Sir Thomas Brown
English Author (1605-1682)

August 22

Birthday of Claude Debussy (1862-1918)

"There is nothing more musical than a sunset. He who feels what he sees will find no more beautiful example of development in all that book which, alas, musicians read but too little - the book of Nature."

Claude Debussy

August 23

"Our fears for today, our worries for tomorrow, and even
the powers of hell can't keep God's love away."

Romans 8:38
The Bible

August 24

"There are more love songs than anything else.
If songs could make you do something, we'd all love one another."

Frank Zappa

August 25

"The most important of the ten commandments is this: Love the Lord your God with all your heart and with all your soul and with all your mind and with all your strength. The second is this: Love your neighbor as yourself. There is no commandment greater than these.'"

Matthew 12:29-31
The Bible

August 26

"Neither a lofty degree of intelligence nor imagination nor both together go to the making of genius. Love, love, love, that is the soul of genius."

Wolfgang Amadeus Mozart

August 27

"Be joyful always; pray continually; give thanks in all circumstances, for this is God's will for you in Christ Jesus." (I Thessalonians 5:16-18, NIV) Did you know that it is God's will for you to be joyful always? God wants you to be happy and carefree. He wants you to love your life no matter what your circumstances look like. In fact, when you have joy in the midst of difficult circumstances, it's evidence of your faith and trust that God is going to bring you through. Understand that God's supernatural joy is His strength. He wants you to have joy so that you can stand strong no matter what's going on around you. You might say, 'Joel, I'm just not a real jovial person. I'm more serious. I never laugh that much.' I realize God made us all differently, but you can train yourself to laugh more. I read where the average child laughs over 200 times a day, but the average adult only laughs 4 times a day. What's happened? We've allowed the pressures of life, stress, and more responsibilities, little by little, to steal our joy."

Joel Osteen

August 28

Birthday of Johann Wolfgang von Goethe (1749-1832)
"In music the dignity of art seems to find supreme expression. There is no subject matter to be discounted. It is all form and significant content. It elevates and ennobles whatever it expresses."

Johann Wolfgang von Goethe
German Writer and Philosopher (1749-1832)

August 29

"Some people say that Beethoven, while writing his symphonies, gave himself up to exalted sentiments - lofty thoughts of God, immortality, and the course of the stars . . . Whereas genius, while pointing to the heavens with its leafy crown, spreads its roots deeply in its beloved earth."

Robert Schumann

August 30

"Beethoven's *Symphony No. 9* seems to contain the different genres of poetry, the first movement being epic, the second, comedy, the third, lyric, the fourth (combining all), the dramatic. Still another bluntly began to praise Symphony 9 as being gigantic, colossal, comparable to the Egyptian pyramids. And others painted word pictures: the symphony expresses the story of mankind: first the chaos - then the call of God 'there shall be light,' - then the sunrise over the first human being, ravished by such splendour. In one word, the whole first chapter of the Hebrew Bible (Pentateuch) is in this Symphony."

Robert Schumann

August 31

"Art was not created as a way to riches. Strive to become a true artist; all else will take care of itself."

Robert Schumann

September

Oriental "Pink Grass" in our Yard

September 1

"Now is the time to restore the rightful place of music education in the lives of our children and in all of our lives."

Don and Delayna Beattie

September 2

"When you grow older, avoid playing what is merely fashionable. Time is precious. It would require a hundred lives merely to get acquainted with all the good music that exists."

Robert Schumann

September 3

"When the power of love overcomes the love of power,
the world will know peace."

Jimi Hendrix
Guitarist Songwriter, Singer (1942-1970)

September 4

'You must gradually learn to know all the most important works
of all the important masters."

Robert Schumann

September 5

"Try to play easy pieces well;
it is better than to play difficult ones poorly."

Robert Schumann

September 6

"You music practice scales and other finger exercises industriously. There are people, however, who think they may achieve great ends by doing this; up to an advanced age, for many hours daily, they practice mechanical exercises. That is as reasonable as trying to recite the alphabet faster and faster every day. Find a better use for your time."

Robert Schumann

September 7

"What do we mean by being musical? You are not so when, with eyes painfully fixed on the notes, you struggle through a piece; you are not so when you stop short and find it impossible for you to proceed because someone has turned over two pages at once. But you are musical when, in playing a new piece, you almost foresee what is coming; when you play an old one by heart; in short, when you have taken music not only into your fingers, but into your heart and head."

Robert Schumann

September 8

"Preoccupation with the execution often prevents one from hearing what one is doing. A technique which by its ease can be guided by the delight of listening becomes the only good piano technique."

Paul Roes

September 9

"To raise a finger in order to strike a piano key may seem at first the necessary requirement for piano playing. But what appears logical in theory may often prove false in practice. Repeat this simple movement; you will see that it becomes fatiguing and that you have recourse to other means for the power to continue it."

Franz Liszt

September 10

"Chopin taught that the fingers are only pillars of support in proper piano technique. Liszt taught that, unlike keyboard technique for the harpsichord that preceded the invention of the piano, one doesn't play the piano only with fingers but with fingers, hands, wrists, forearms, shoulders, torso, heart, soul and all of one's being" With Liszt having been the most illustrious pupil of Carl Czerny who, in turn, was the most illustrious pupil of Beethoven, it is fitting that Reginald Gerig, in his book, "Famous Pianists and Their Technique," called Beethoven "the first of the great pianists."

Franz Liszt
Paul Roes

September 11

"A student could say: 'I must say to you that it upsets me to think that thousands of piano students are thus handicapped or even doomed to failure (because of playing by raising the fingers). I begin to catch a glimpse of a new method.' The teacher replies: 'It is nothing new. Beethoven, Liszt and Chopin played in this only valid manner, but one loses sight of it. Chopin would not have become a great pianist if he had not followed the natural laws.'"

Paul Roes

September 12

In 1880, Diepenbrock said "A time will come when a word will have become the replacement for its' own significance. For those who thus label the things of the soul, music remains a dead language."

Alphons Diepenbrock
Dutch Composer and Essayist (1862-1921)

September 13

One master said to his students: "My friends, there are no scales. Neither are there octaves, nor fifths, nor thirds. There are only intervals between two voices. It is as if I spoke to you and you answered me."

Paul Roes

September 14

In the house of Prince Lichnowsky, a Hungarian count once laid before Beethoven a difficult composition by Bach, in manuscript, which Beethoven performed with great readiness at sight. One day a musician by the name of Forster brought Beethoven a quartet, which he had copied out only that morning. In the second part of the first movement, the cellist left. Beethoven stood up and, while continuing to play his piano part, sang the bass accompaniment. To a friend who expressed his wonder at this through knowledge, Beethoven said, smiling, "So the bass part had to be, else the author understood nothing of composition." Whereupon the author remarked that Beethoven had played the piano part at presto, which he had never seen before, so fast that it would have impossible to see the single notes. "That is not necessary," replied Beethoven. "If you read rapidly, you may not see nor heed them, if only you know the language."

Ludwig van Beethoven

September 15

In his book, *"Beethoven: His Spiritual Development,"* J.W. N. Sullivan wrote. "To Beethoven, music was not only a manifestation of the beautiful, an art, it was akin to religion. He felt himself to be a prophet, a seer." And in a letter Beethoven wrote to a ten-year-old admirer, Emile M., on July 17, 1812: "Go on; do not practice art alone but penetrate to her heart; she deserves it, for art and science only can raise man to Godhood."

Ludwig van Beethoven
J.W.N. Sullivan

September 16

Beethoven's poignant spiritual testimony is quoted by Bettina von Arnim in a letter to Goethe: "I have not a single friend; I must live alone. But well I know that God is nearer to me than others artists; I associate with him without fear; I have always recognized and understood Him and have no fear for my music - its fate cannot be other than happy; whoever succeeds in grasping it shall be absolved from all the misery that bows down other men."

Ludwig van Beethoven

September 17

From James Agee's *"Let Us Now Praise Famous Men,"* published in 1939: "Beethoven said a thing as rash and noble as the best of his work. By my memory, he said, 'He who understands my music can never again know unhappiness.' I believe it. What is art for? It is to heal men's souls by a revelation. But this revelation can never be convincing if it conceals or denies the pain over which it triumphs. Rising courageously above the misery that is most men's lot, its intoxicating message of beauty, humor, and joy is a moral proposition demanding creative participation to be effective therapy."

James Agee
American Novelist, Journalist, Poet (1909-1955)

September 18

"Liszt does not play for others but for himself. He depicts his own feelings, he expresses his own soul, and it is probably the best way to reach the soul of his literature."

Paul Roes

September 19

"When you think you are practicing slowly . . . Slow down some more," Liszt said. "You spoil everything if you want to cut corners. Nature itself works quietly. Do likewise. Take it easy. If conducted wisely, your efforts will be crowned with success. If you hurry, they will be wasted and you will fail."

Franz Liszt

September 20

Author Walter Hubbe, from *"Brahms in Hamburg,"* writes, "Brahms never aimed at mere effect, but seemed to plunge into the innermost meaning of whatever music he happened to be interpreting, exhibiting all its details, and expressing its very depths. Brahms did not play like a consummately trained, highly intelligent musician making other people's works his own but rather like one who was himself creating, who interpreted the composer's works as an equal, not merely reproducing them, but rendering them as if they gushed forth directly and powerfully from his heart."

Johannes Brahms
German Composer and Pianist (1833-1897)

September 21

"Frequently at the close of lessons, Brahms would perform many of the Bach Preludes and Fugues. His students were particularly struck by the emotional, poetic qualities of his Bach playing."

Reginald Gerig

September 22

In his later years, the great cellist, Pablo Casals, would go to the piano each morning and play a Bach Prelude and Fugue. He said that "he felt it brought a blessing onto his home."

Pablo Casals

September 23

"As you grow older, converse more frequently with scores than with virtuosos. Industriously practice the fugues of good masters; above all, those of J.S. Bach. Let 'The Well-tempered Clavichord' be your daily meat. Then you will certainly become an able musician."

Robert Schumann

September 24

"There is one source which is inexhaustibly provides new ideas - Johann Sebastian Bach. . . In fact, to my mind, Bach is un approachable - his is unfathomable."

Robert Schumann

September 25

Birthday of Glenn Gould (1932-1982)
"I think that if I were required to spend the rest of my life on a desert island, and to listen to or play the music of any once composer during all that time, that composer would almost certainly be J. S. Bach. I really can't think of any other music which is so all-encompassing, which moves me so deeply and so consistently, and which, to use a rather imprecise word, is valuable beyond all of its skill and brilliance for something more meaningful than that - its humanity."

Glenn Gould
Canadian Pianist (1932-1982)

September 26

Birthday of George Gershwin (1898-1937)
"I didn't even start playing the piano until I was about 13 or 14. I guess I

must have had a little talent or whatever-you-call-it, but I practiced regularly, and that's what counts."

George Gershwin
American Composer and Pianist (1898-1937)

September 27

"Life is a lot like jazz . . . It's best when you improvise."

George Gershwin

September 28

"The man who looks at a canvas or listens to music is passive, but he is passive only to the extent that he is unable to create. For in listening to the music he is active; he is going through the same needs of expression, and the same self-projection, that the creator went through. It has been repeatedly said that the listener likes the music in which he finds himself, in which he recognizes his own emotions and tastes."

Carlos Chavez
Mexican Composer and Conductor (1899-1978)

September 29

Having attended a Liszt recital in Paris in 1835, Henry Reeves wrote, "Liszt had already played a great fantasia of his own, and Beethoven's Opus 90 Piano Sonata. After this latter piece, he gasped with emotion as I shook his hand and thanked him for the divine energy he had shed forth. As the closing strains began, Mendelssohn's *"Chants san paroles,"* I saw Liszt's countenance assume that agony of expression, mingled with radiant smiles of joy, which I never saw in any other human face except in the paintings of Our Saviour by some of the early masters."

Franz Liszt

September 30

"There are souls in this world which have the gift of finding joy everywhere, and leaving it behind them when they go."

Frederick William Faber
English Hymn Writer and Theologian (1814-1863)

October

View Under the Train Trestle in Jewell, Iowa

October 1
Birthday of Vladimir Horowitz (1903-1989)
"Everyone goes to the forest; some go for a walk to be inspired,
and others go to cut down the trees."

Vladimir Horowitz

October 2
"Young and old composers, there is one thing you may learn from it of
which, above all things, it is necessary to remind you -
Nature, Nature, Nature!"

Robert Schumann

October 3
"The woods would be very silent if no birds sang
except those that sang best."

Henry David Thoreau
American Philosopher, Journalist, Poet (1817-1862)

October 4

"As you listen to the lucid and lovely music of Beethoven's Symphony No. 6 'Pastoral,' full of sincerity, candor and sweet gravity, you may recall the folk tale of the old man. He could always be found at sunrise looking seaward through the shadow of the woods, with his white locks blowing in the wind that rose out of the dawn; and who, being asked why he was not at his prayers, replied; 'Every morning like this, I take off my hat to the beauty of the world.'"

Lawrence Gilman
American Author and Music Critic (1878-1939)

October 5

Only Children Live There
"One must become a child again to enter the Kingdom of Heaven"

"A great city that I saw, with a diamond waterfall,
Rooms hide in the cliffs above, to be tall and live there,
A great city in the woods, miracles if understood,
A green village underfoot, to be small and live there,
Look out, look up, look down, She's there, out there,
It's taken me so long, to greet you.
More trees than could have a name, no two days are they the same,
They've seen more than you or I, to be old and live there,
Water rushing tells a tale, little friends are setting sail,
Each day something special born, to be young and live there,
Just see, just hear, just feel, be glad, it's real,
I now know why you're called, a Kingdom.
My hat is off to you, to praise, your blue,
There is no finer green, to be seen.
A Kingdom before my eyes, your beauty I realize,
Is home if we take the time, to be wise and live there,
A great city all around, her borders span ev'ry town,
All people are welcome though, only children live there,
Look out, look up, look down, She's there, out there,
It's taken me so long, to greet you,
The birds are singing praise, their songs, amaze,
It's taken me so long, to hear you.
A great city that I saw, with a diamond waterfall,
Rooms hide in the cliffs above, to be tall and live there,
A great city in the woods, miracles if understood,
A green village underfoot, to be small and live there,
To be young and live there, only children live there."

Donald Beattie
c. 1996 Edition HAS Music Publishing Co.

October 6

"Go confidently in the direction of your dreams.
Live the life you have imagined."

Henry David Thoreau

October 7

"Imagination derives from the phrase 'image of a nation.' How each of us see the world is each of our imagination. Music is derived from the word 'muse' which means to think. As mind and heart are not separate, the mind expresses the love of heart. Music is listening from the heart and expression of feeling in sound. With our feelings and imagination, 'image of the world,' we make music."

Don and Delayna Beattie

October 8

"How do you know when you're serving God from your heart? The first telltale sign is enthusiasm. When you're doing what you love to do, no one has to motivate you, or challenge you, or check up on you. You do it for the sheer enjoyment. You don't need rewards, or applause, or to be paid, because you love serving in this way. The opposite is also true: When you don't have a heart for what you're doing, you're easily discouraged."

Rick Warren

October 9

"William James said, 'The best use of your life is to spend it for something that outlasts it.' . . . There are people on this planet whom only you will be able to reach, because of where you live and what God has made you to be. If just one person will be in heaven because of you, your life will have made a difference for eternity."

Rick Warren

October 10

"Straight away the ideas flow in upon me, directly from God, and not only do I see distinct themes in my mind's eye, but they are clothed in the right forms, harmonies and orchestration."

Johannes Brahms

October 11

"When Beethoven gave me a lesson he was, I might almost say, unnaturally patient. This, as well as his friendly treatment of me, which very seldom varied, I must ascribe principally to his attachment and love for my father. Thus he often would have me repeat a single number ten or more times. In Beethoven's Variations in F Major, opus 34, I was obliged to repeat almost the entire final Adagio variation seventeen times in a lesson with Beethoven. Even then, Beethoven was not satisfied with the expression in the small cadenza. When I left out something in a passage, a note or a skip, or struck a wrong key, he seldom said anything; yet when I was at fault with regard to the expression, the crescendo or matter of that kind, or in the character of the piece, he would grow angry. Mistakes of the other kind, he said, were due to chance; but these last resulted from want of knowledge, feeling or attention. He himself often made mistakes of the first kind, even when playing in public."

Ferdinand Ries
German Composer and Friend, Pupil and Secretary of Beethoven
(1784-1838)

October 12

In a letter to Carl Czerny, Vienna, 1817, Beethoven wrote about lessons for his nephew, Karl: "Please be as patient as possible with our Karl, even though at present he may not be making as much progress as you and I would like. If you are not patient, he will do even less well, because (although he must not know this) owing to the unsatisfactory timetable for his lessons, he is being unduly strained. Unfortunately nothing can be done about that for the time being. Treat him, therefore so far as possible, with affection, but be firm with him. Then there will be a greater chance of success in spite of these really unfavorable circumstances where Karl is concerned - In regard to his playing for you, as soon as he has learnt the right fingering and can play a piece in correct time and the notes are more or less accurately, then please check him only about his interpretation: and when he has reached that point, don't let him stop playing for the sake of minor mistakes, but point them out to him when he has finished playing the piece. Although I have done very little teaching, yet I have always followed this method. It soon produces musicians which, after all, is one of the chief aims of the art."

Ludwig van Beethoven

October 13

My Friend
for Delayna

"While it's midnight, there's a light inside of me because of you,
Love is timeless, there's no measure for the love I feel for you.
I will say a prayer for you, in this quiet way with you,
While there may be miles between me and your smile,
I see your face tonight.
I will say my prayers for you, I will share my dreams with you,
Let our spirits fly to the heavens on high, I'll meet you there tonight.
While it's midnight, there's a light inside of me because of you,
Love is timeless, there's no measure for the love I feel for you.
The love I feel for you, My Friend."

Donald Beattie, composed May, 1993
c. 1996 Edition Has Music Publishing Co.

October 14

"Happy is the man who finds a true friend,
and far happier is he who finds that true friend in his wife."

Franz Schubert

October 15

"Friends are not only together when they are side by side.
Even one who is far away is still in our thoughts."

Ludwig van Beethoven

October 16

Liszt taught by suggestion in advising
"Follow yourself the road that I can only point but to you."

Franz Liszt

October 17

"Bach is like an astronomer who, with the help of ciphers, finds the most wonderful stars . . . Beethoven embraced the universe with the power of his spirit . . . I do not climb so high. A long time ago I decided that my universe will be the soul and heart of man."

Frederic Chopin

October 18

"Beethoven learned directly from Clementi how, after searching everywhere for positive rules governing performance, he finally found the key in vocal art. Himself a singer, he attempted to apply the rules of prosody even to certain instrumental passages where stressed and unstressed notes in endless sequence played an important role."

Anton Schindler

October 19

"As for Beethoven's particular style of accentuation, the author (Schindler) can speak partly from Beethoven's critical remarks on Czerny's playing and partly from the piano instruction that Beethoven gave to him directly. It was above all the rhythmic accent that he stressed most heavily and that he wanted others to stress. He treated the melodic (or grammatic, as it was generally called) accent, on the other hand, mostly according to the internal requirements. Beethoven would emphasize all retardations, especially that of the diminished second in cantabile sections, more than other pianists. His playing thus acquired a highly personal character, very different from the even, flat performances that never rise to tonal eloquence. In cantilena sections, he adopted the methods of cultivated singers, doing neither too much nor too little. Sometimes he recommended putting appropriate words to a perplexing passage and singing it, or listening to a good violinist or wind player play it."

Anton Schindler

October 20

"Music resembles chess. The queen (melody) has the greatest power,
but the king (harmony) decides the game."

Robert Schumann

October 21

"The study of the history of music and the hearing of masterworks of
different epochs will speediest of all cure you
of vanity and self-adoration."

Robert Schumann

October 22

Birthday of Franz Liszt (1811-1886)

"Supreme serenity still remains the Ideal of great Art. The shapes and transitory forms of life are but stages toward this Ideal, which Christ's religion illuminates with His Divine Light."

Franz Liszt

October 23

"Chopin's music was spontaneous, miraculous. He found it without seeking it, without previous intimation of it. It came upon his piano sudden, complete, sublime, or it sang in his head during a walk, and he was impatient to hear it himself with the help of the instrument. But then began the most desperate labor and I have ever witnessed. It was a succession of efforts, hesitations, and moments of impatience to recapture certain details of the theme he could hear; what he had conceived as one piece, he analyzed too much in trying to write it down, and his dismay at his inability to rediscover it in what he thought was its original purity threw him into a kind of despair. He would lock himself up in his room for whole days, weeping, pacing back and forth, breaking his pens, repeating or changing one bar a hundred times, writing and erasing it as many times, and beginning again the next day with an infinite and desperate perseverance. He sometimes spent six weeks on one page, only in the end to write it exactly as he had sketched at the first draft."

Armantine Lucile Dupin "George Sand"
French Novelist (1804-1876)

October 24

"Chopin has written two wonderful mazurkas which are worth more than forty novels and are more eloquent than the entire century's literature."

George Sand

October 25

"God is far more interested in what you are than what you do. We are human beings not human doings. Remember, you will take your character into eternity, but not your career. Peter said, 'Don't lose a minute in building on what you've been given, complementing your basic faith with good character, spiritual understanding, alert discipline, passionate patience, reverent wonder, warm friendliness, and generous love.' It takes a lifetime to build Christ like character."

Rick Warren

October 26

"I think house-music is at its highest conceivable level when amateurs mix with professionals, all doing it for love . . . The German audiences in the medium-sized towns were composed of people who loved music unselfishly. They knew most of the music they went to hear at concerts. They knew it very well. There was probably not one in these audiences who was not involved, actively or passively, in home-made music – and without any fuss made about it. It was part of family life, old and young co-operating. The children were present and listened. Public concerts especially for children did not yet exist: youngsters deeply attracted to music simply attended some concerts."

Artur Schnabel
Austrian Classical Pianist and Teacher (1882-1951)

October 27

"My lifelong passion for mountaineering and hiking dates from pre-Vienna days, for my birthplace was also surrounded by hills not unlike those adorning Vienna. It is not too easy in America to satisfy this passion. Of all human beings the most ignored in the States seems to be he who walks out of love, just for the joy in walking. I nevertheless tried. The four summers I spent in New Mexico were most enjoyable though very different from my European experiences. Cattle, horses and wood-cutters were responsible for trails which took weeks to discover. And in four summers of walking in the woods there, every day for at least eight miles, I never met a single soul. True, it was a remote and unknown place, and no sightseers, motorists or tourists ever approached it. Yet, there were villages and city close to them. I went another summer to Colorado's very, very beautiful mountains, woods and lakes."

Artur Schnabel

October 28

"It was the habit of Brahms every Sunday morning of the spring and autumn season to make an excursion (if the weather permitted) into the lovely hilly woods surrounding Vienna. He was accompanied by a few friends, chiefly musicians. When I was twelve or thirteen, a friend thought me old enough to join them once in a while. I thus enjoyed the unique privilege of spending several Sundays as a boy with Brahms and his companions."

Artur Schnabel

October 29

"I am attracted only to music which I consider to be better than it can be performed . . . His whole life, his whole conversation, was unending discovery and the whole of his teaching was bent to one end: to make pupils think for themselves."

Artur Schnabel

October 30

"When he played the piano, Schnabel did not move his arms, his hands, except to get them from one part of the keyboard to another. He did not bend over the keys. He sat, quite relaxed, not on a stool but on a special high-backed chair, leaning as a rule slightly back: a series of immensely thundering octaves would be produced with no more apparent expenditure of physical effort than a single note, played contemplatively, *piano*. . . His pauses were organic: through them the music breathed. When he played the *arietta* of Beethoven's Opus 111 Piano Sonata, time stood still. . . Many of the most distinguished colleagues and swiftly growing audiences were moved to tears by the unsurpassed profundity of controlled emotion evoked by that small, still figure."

Edward Crankshaw, Editor
"Artur Schnabel. My life and Music"

October 31

"It may well be, I submit, that the more one is inclined, or seduced, to possess, conserve and enjoy materials things, the less one may have to give in the personal exchange of souls, minds and brains. . . Real happiness will perhaps then only be established in human beings when much will be expected from their inner qualities and higher potentialities."

Artur Schnabel

Don and Delayna Beattie

November

The John P. Cable Grist Mill in Cades Cove
in the Great Smoky Mountain National Park

November 1

"Music does bring people together. It allows us to experience the same emotions. People everywhere are the same in heart and spirit. No matter what language we speak, what color we are, the form of our politics or the expression of our love and our faith, music proves: We are the same."

John Denver
Musician, Singer-Songwriter, Humanitarian (1943-1997)

November 2

"I would so much like young people to have a sense of the gift that they are. Not many of them feel like that."

John Denver

November 3

"My purpose in performing is to communicate the joy
I experience in living."

John Denver

November 4

The original symbolism of solfege tones in a descending major scale:

DO	DOminus *(God the Father)*
TI	Originally called SI - SIdera *(all star systems, universe)*
LA	LActea *(Milky Way, our galaxy)*
SOL	SOL *(our sun, head of the solar system)*
FA	FAta *(Fate)*
MI	MIcrocosmos *(small world, or man upon the earth)*
RE	REgina de Coeli *(Queen of the Heavens, the moon)*
DO	DOminus *(God the Father)*

"As mathematician, Pythagoras measured distances between the seven known planetary bodies of his time. Further, he measured the speed of the tonal vibrations of each of the seven tones in the major (Ionian) scale. He discovered that proportionally, the ratio of vibrations between the seven scale tones mirrored the distances between the seven planetary bodies. His teachings further examined what came to be known as *"music of the spheres."* Consideration of the seven days of the week, the seven energy centers (chakras) of our bodies and the seven days of Creation give an ever deepening appreciation for the profundity of the seven tone major scale of the Western Music system. To be certain, composers of the stature of Bach, Mozart and Beethoven were intimately aware of the teachings of Pythagoras and other philosophers teachings with their music compositions profoundly influenced by the deep spiritual meaning of the language of music. In short, a descent through the tones of the scale, is a descent from God, our Universe, our Galaxy, our Sun, our Fate, ourselves, our Moon and to God again."

Pythagoras
Mathematician, Musician and Mystic (570-495BC)
Herbert Whone
English Violinist, Teacher, Painter (1925-2011)

November 5

"Music has the capacity of redeemer. It is the rediscovery of our common Source through the attuning of our vibrations, of our words and sound to the Divine Word and through the agency of harmony and healing in our music. Thus it is said, 'music is the handmaid of religion.' This idea is even more transparent in the nature and symbolism of the seven-tone (major, Ionian) scale, and the Western harmonic system. Man's existence on earth is not simply for his benefit, but for the purpose of being an agent in the Divine plan for Self-Realization - an idea that rings through all ancient teachings. That is, in serving himself, man serves God: he is God's instrument. . . Not the archetypal seven-fold strutting, the expression of Absolute Power, is seen as a descending octave. Such an octave, consisting of a cosmic hierarchy is disguised in the innocuous DO, SI, LA, SOL, FA, MI RE of the so-called tonic-fa system. Originating in the monastic tradition of the twelfth century, the names are said to have arisen as a mere convenience for singers; however, their true significance, though there are other interpretations, lies in the following Latin words: Dominus (God the Father), Sidera (star systems), Lactea (Milky Way - our galaxy), SOL (our sun - head of the solar system), Fata (Fate, or the planetary net), Microcosmos (small world or man upon the earth), and Regina de Coeli (Queen of the Heavens, the moon). The semitone point between MI and FA is the place of man's true 'work' - his spiritual work - with the semitone point between SI (TI) and Do being man's opportunity to reach God. . . Man creates his own ascending scale; this is his aspiration. . . Thus it is that in music, he responds inwardly to every small rise and fall in direction. It seems too simple yet this is his underlying response in the whole of music; through music, he is moved upwards and downwards in that contradiction in his soul, a dynamic play of opposites."

Herbert Whone
from "Music, The Way of Return"

November 6

All the Lovely Way Home

"Do Sol Re, means to me, special notions of what we can be,
In your way, sing with me, music's motion will help set us free,
Look, look to the stars, they will reflect, all that we are,
Evening by the sea, beautiful waves, singing for thee,
Help to sing this song, it won't take long,
Music shows us all the lovely way home.
Do Sol Re, you can play, traveling round the world in just one day,
Image of music's love, with imagination of above,
Moon, whispers to me telling of family she sees,
Sun, he waits above, patiently shining, he's in love,
Help to sing this song, it won't take long,
Music shows us all the lovely way home.

Do Sol Re, Re Sol Mi, Do Sol Fa Mi Re Sol La Ti Do,
Do Sol Re, Re Sol Mi, Do Sol Fa Mi Re Sol La Ti Do,
Just these little words, like little birds, show us on high,
Yes, these special tones, know the way home, to deep inside,
As my voice fades, hear this song in your heart,
Thanks to music, we are never apart,
I will sing this song, it won't take long,
Music shows us all the lovely way home,
All the lovely way home, all the lovely way home."

Donald Beattie
c. 1993 Edition HAS Music
Publishing Co.

November 7

Birthday of Billy Graham (1918 -)

"Franz Joseph Haydn, the great musician, was once asked why his church music was so cheerful. He replied, 'When I think upon God, my heart is so full of joy that the notes dance and leap, as it were, from my pen, and since God has given me a cheerful heart, it will be pardoned me that I serve Him with a cheerful spirit.' Haydn had discovered the secret to lasting joy: 'I think on God.' Looking at our circumstances won't bring us lasting joy. It may even make us depressed or angry. But when we think on God, when we turn our minds and hearts to His power and His love for us, we can't help but be joyful. Paul said 'Set your minds above not on things on earth.' (Col. 3:2). Discouragement flees in the face of joy."

Billy Graham

November 8

The word emotion comes from "energy in motion." In the twentieth century, physicists determined that everything, all matter is comprised of energy in motion - the universe, the planets, ourselves and all of life - and music. As the strings of a piano vibrate, as the music we play at the piano vibrates and as we connect to music and our instrument with our own vibrations, something beautiful, unseen and harmonious can occur. It is this unseen reality that begins to shed light on the reality of the soul, the spirit, the heart and the profundity and power of the living spiritual language of music.

Don and Delayna Beattie

November 9

"For a satisfying concert performance, consider how many circumstances must favorably unite before the beautiful can emerge in all its dignity and splendor. We need lofty, serious intention and great ideality; enthusiasm in presentation; virtuosity of workmanship and harmonic cooperation; inner desire and need of the give and the received; momentarily favorable mood in audience and artist alike; a fortunate combination of time, place, and general conditions, as well as of the auspicious moment; direction and communication of impressions, feelings, views; a reflection of the joy of art in the eyes of others. Is not such a combination a happy throw with six dice of sixes!"

Robert Schumann

November 10

"The supreme happiness of life," Victor Hugo said, "is the conviction that we are loved." "Love is the first requirement for mental health," declared Sigmund Freud. All should learn and play music as it is love."

Billy Graham

November 11

"As a young boy, I would often see a white haired, elderly married couple who were music teachers and wherever they went, they were holding hands. Without knowing it, they were a great inspiration to me and my future marriage to my wife, Ruth."

Billy Graham

November 12

"It doesn't matter where you go in life, it's who you have beside you."

Author unknown

November 13

"In his improvisations, even then Beethoven did not deny his tendency toward the mysterious and gloomy. When once he began to revel in the infinite world of tones, he was transported also above all earthly things - his spirit had burst all restricting bonds, shaken off the yoke of servitude and soared triumphantly and jubilantly into the luminous spaces of the higher ether. Now his playing tore along with a wildly foaming cataract, and the conjurer constrained his instrument to an utterance so forceful that the stoutest structure was scarcely able to withstand it. . . Again, Beethoven's spirit would soar aloft, triumphing over transitory terrestrial sufferings, turn its glance upward in reverent sounds and find rest and comfort on the innocent bosom of holy nature. But who shall sound the depths of the sea?   It was the mystical Sanscrit language whose heiroglyphics can be read only by the initiated."

Ignaz von Seyfried

November 14
Birthday of Aaron Copland (1900-1990)
"So long as the human spirit thrives on this planet, music, in some living form, will accompany and sustain it and give it expressive meaning."

Aaron Copland

November 15
"The love of one's country is a splendid thing.
But why should love stop at the border?"

Pablo Casals

November 16
"Pianists Play All 9 Symphonies by Beethoven Back-to-Back"
"It took 26 pianists, playing in relays, most of a day and an evening, but the 'Beethoven Experience of a Lifetime' ended successfully despite a power failure and some nervous dancers. For Donald Beattie, director of Carbondale's Beethoven Society, the April 23rd back-to-back performance of all nine symphonies by Ludwig van Beethoven capped two years of planning and months of rehearsal. The extravaganza at Southern Illinois University's Shryock auditorium was held to raise US$25,000 to buy six new pianos for the university's School of Music, and those with the stamina to sit through the full 13 hours got their money's worth.

They heard all nine symphonies in piano reduction, with a bit of dance thrown in for eye appeal during the Fifth Symphony, and then in the evening heard the Fifth again in orchestral form - plus two Beethoven concerti. For most of the marathon, one solo pianist sat in the center of the stage, while two or sometimes four pianists worked at the left and the right playing together at two or three grand pianos. Beattie played the Franz Liszt solo piano reductions in four of the symphonies and played a part in all nine symphony performances. The grand finale brought out the resources of the Illinois Arts Trio and the Southern Illinois University Symphony Orchestra for the full-score version of the Fifth and the concerti.

The day long concert began at 9 am and continued with a symphony an hour through the day. According to the performers, it was fairly smooth sailing through the youthful First and Second Symphonies, the revolutionary Third, or 'Eroica,' and the seldom-performed Fourth. The mighty Fifth, however, presented some problems because organizers thought the 1000 elementary school children then in the auditorium would enjoy it more if there were dancing. They brought in the 'Dance Repertory Group,' led by Toni Intravaia, who remarked afterwards: 'Beethoven need not be danced. I think Beethoven is complete in himself.' The eight dancers had a strip of only 7 feet (2 meters) to work in between the pianos and the stage apron.

There were no special problems in the flowing No. 6, or 'Pastorale,' but potential disaster hit with the complete Seventh Symphony. As No. 7 began, a campus-wide power outage struck, leaving a trio of pianists, including Beattie, in dim light and without amplification. 'We went on in the spirit of Beethoven,' Beattie said. Power was restored in time for No. 8 and the pianists' greatest challenge, the long and celebrated Ninth.

Beattie said he knows of no other successful attempts to stage such a Beethoven marathon. A social club organized by the late H.L. Mencken once attempted the feat in a Baltimore parlor, but Mencken's account has it that many of the musicians succumbed to the effects of beer before reaching the final chorale of the Ninth."

Associated Press
The China Post. Taiwan. April 25, 1987

November 17

"When you play, do not concern yourself with who may be listening."

Robert Schumann

November 18

"No children can be brought to healthy manhood on sweet-meats and pastry. Spiritual like bodily nourishment must be simple and solid. The masters have provided it; cleave to them."

Robert Schumann

November 19

"It is very nice indeed if you can pick out little melodies on the keyboard; but if such come spontaneously to you, and not at the pianoforte, rejoice even more, for it proves that your inner sense of tone is awakening. Fingers must do what the head wells; not vice versa."

Robert Schumann

November 20

"He who is too eager to preserve his originality
is already in the course of losing it."

Robert Schumann

November 21

"Above all things, persevere in composing mentally, not with the help of the instrument, and keep on twisting and turning the principal melodies about in your head until you can say to yourself: 'Now they work.' To hit upon the right thing all in a moment, as it were, does not happen every day, and the sketchbooks of great composers, especially of Beethoven, prove how long and how laboriously they often worked over a simple melody and kept on improving upon it."

Robert Schumann

November 22

In 1814, Beethoven made his second complete version of *"Fidelio"* with the very practical help of Treitschke. The poet has left a vivid description of one episode of their collaboration, his rewriting of Florestan's Aria: "What I am now relating will remain always in my memory. Beethoven read it, ran up and down the room, muttered, growled, as was his habit instead of singing, and tore open the pianoforte. My wife had often begged Beethoven to play; today he placed the text in front of him and began to improvise marvelously - music which no magic could hold fast. Out of it, he seemed to conjure the motive of the aria. The hours went by, but Beethoven improvised on. Supper, which he had intended to eat with us, was served, but he would not be disturbed. It was late when he embraced me, and declining the meal, hurried home. The next day, the admirable composition was finished."

Georg Friedrich Treitschke
German Poet and Librettist (1776-1842)

November 23

Ignaz von Seyfried, a contemporary conductor, described Beethoven's lodgings: "A truly admirable confusion ruled in his household. Books and music were strewn about in every corner; here the fragments of a cold snack, there bottles, still sealed or half emptied; on his standing desk was the hurried sketch of a new quartet; elsewhere were the debris of his breakfast; here on the piano, in the shape of scribbled-over pages, lay the material for a magnificent symphony, still slumbering as an embryo; there drooped a corrected proof waiting for release. The floor was covered with business and personal letters; between the windows stood a respectable loaf of Strachino, beside it the still notable ruins of a genuine Verona salami. How could any of these things trouble this man filled with a sacred fire, who bore God in his heart."

Ignaz von Seyfried

November 24
Young Ferdinand Ries wrote: "Beethoven was very clumsy and awkward in his movements; his gestures were totally lacking in grace. He seldom took up anything without dropping it and breaking it. Thus he repeatedly threw his inkwell into the piano that stood next to his writing desk. No piece of furniture was safe, least of all a valuable one; everything was knocked over, dirtied and destroyed. How he ever managed to shave himself is hard to understand, even making all allowance for the many cuts on his cheeks. And he never learned to dance in time to music."

Ferdinand Ries

November 25
"In my days of deafness, I almost reached the point of putting an end to my life - only art it was that held me back, ah, it seemed impossible to leave the world until I had brought forth all that I felt called upon to produce . . . Forced already in my 28th year to become a philosopher, O, it is not easy, and harder for an artist than another - God, thou lookest into my inmost being, thou knowest that love of man and desire to do good live in me . . . Recommend virtue to your children, it alone can give happiness, not money, I speak from experience . . . The high courage - which often inspired me in the beautiful days of summer - has disappeared - O God - grant me at least but one day of pure joy - it is so long since real joy has echoed in my heart - O when - O when - O Divine One - shall I feel it again in the temple of nature and of men."

Ludwig van Beethoven
from the "Heiligenstadt Testament"
October 6, 1802

November 26
"The term, 'tempo modification,' (is) the result of a desire to give musical ideas a spontaneous, speaking quality, as though one were telling a story or delivering a speech. If I habitually think in terms of notes and bar lines and do not recognize musical ideas or sense the need to make judgments about derivations and relationships, my playing will always sound unimaginative, and all the contemporary advice in existence will be to no avail.

At the same time, permitting ideas and subjective responses to control one's playing, which apparently accounted for the extraordinary effect Beethoven's playing had upon his listeners, means risking an unevenness in performance that has become generally unacceptable today. Since our image of success is so strongly associated with auditions, degree recitals, contests, and the perfection available through the record player, the thought on an impulse disturbing our composure or conflicting with the opinions of an artistic umpire who will evaluate us encourages the belief that communicating external perfection is more important than communicating ideas . . . Beethoven was concerned with meaning and communicating feelings and ideas."

Kenneth Drake
American Piano Professor, Author and Performer
from "The Sonatas of Beethoven as He Played and Taught Them"

November 27

"The art of interpretation is not to play what is written."
Pablo Casals

November 28

"So much of what Beethoven expresses is unique. Nothing like it can be found elsewhere, either in music or poetry. And yet we regard these unique states as fundamental and greatly prize them. It is as if Beethoven is the one voice that has expressed a certain region of the human soul - states of consciousness that we may call musical in the sense that they have been expressed, and perhaps can be expressed, only by music."
J.W.N. Sullivan

November 29

Beethoven wrote to his music publisher, Schott, in 1824, "What is all this compared with the great Tone Master above! Above! Above! And righteously the Most High, whereas here below, all is mockery, - dwarfs, - and yet Most High!!" From Beethoven's diary, we read, "He who is above, - O He is, and without Him there is nothing." To Frau Streicher, Beethoven said, "Today is Sunday. Shall I read something for you from the Gospels? 'Love ye one another.'"
Ludwig van Beethoven

November 30

Beethoven's most illustrious student, Carl Czerny, taught his own student, Theodore Leschetizky, much about Beethoven's manner of freely interpreting his own sonatas. Czerny taught that Beethoven should be rendered with freedom of delivery and depth of feeling. A pedantic, inelastic interpretation of the master made Czerny wild. Czerny's vocabulary of character, words that Beethoven used in lessons that he taught Czerny, are taken from Czerny's *"Piano School."* The list is by no means complete, yet it gives an idea of the richness of Beethoven's interpretive vocabulary. One thing for certain. For Beethoven and the other great composers, music can surely express far more than "happy" and "sad." In the words of Tchaikovsky, "Music expresses a thousand shifting nuances of feeling of my soul."

unruly	serious	tragic	teasing
weighty	fantastic	humorous	pathetic
lulling	firm	intimate	bewitching
determined	fleeting	complaining	religious
brilliant	joyous	strong	roaring
singing	pious	noisy	peaceful
capriciously	tender	lively	touching
chorale-like	witty	light	gentle
delicate	good-natured	charming	jocose
dramatic	powerful	virile	flattering
exalted	sparkling	marked	dejected
simple	expressively	melancholy	speaking
elegant	graceful	merry	stormy
mournful	shrill	murmuring	agitated
energetic	grand	mischievous	profound
resolute	serene	naïve	dreamy
lofty	heroic	unaffected	sensitive

Carl Czerny
Austrian Composer, Teacher, Pianist (1791-1857)

Don and Delayna Beattie

December

Our Keeshond Jumer

December 1

"The idea and the effort must be firmly joined to the desire that is within us, in order to render our being conscious of its universality, and to develop our individual liberty far from everything artificial. Only the truly harmonious man who has known how to identify his thoughts, his feelings, and his acts with the great forces of nature, is capable of realizing an art in intimate relation with the supreme harmony of the Cosmos, reflected in the supreme harmony of the spirit...One does not play the piano with the fingers nor with the hands, but also with the arms, the back, the heart, the whole being..."

Paul Roes
Franz Liszt

December 2

"There is geometry in the humming of the strings.
There is music in the spacing of the spheres."

Pythagoras

December 3

"Music is the divine way to tell beautiful, poetic things to the heart."

Pablo Casals

December 4

"A musician must make music, an artist must paint, a poet must write,
if he it to be ultimately at peace with himself."

Abraham Maslow
American Psychologist (1908-1970)

December 5

"If you plan on being anything less than you are capable of being,
you will probably be unhappy all the days of your life."

Abraham Maslow

December 6

"What is Music? How do you define it? Music is a calm moonlit night, the rustle of leaves in Summer. Music is the far off peal of bells at dusk! Music comes straight from the heart and talks only to the heart: it is Love! Music is the Sister of Poetry and her Mother is sorrow!"

Sergei Rachmaninoff
Russian Composer and Concert Pianist (1873-1943)

December 7

"Music is enough for a lifetime, but a lifetime is not enough for music."

Sergei Rachmaninoff

December 8

In 1810, Beethoven said to Bettina von Arnim, "From the focus of enthusiasm, I must discharge melody in all directions: I pursue it, capture it again passionately, I see it flying away and disappearing in the mass of varied agitations; now I seize upon it again with renewed passion; I cannot tear myself from it; I am impelled with hurried modulations to multiply it, and, at length, I conquer it - behold, a symphony!" Beethoven, unlike many composers, was always certain of his goal when composing and rarely made changes in a finished work. In a letter dated February, 1813, to George Thomson, Beethoven wrote, "I am not in the habit of rewriting my compositions. I never did it because I am profoundly convinced that every change of detail changes the character of the whole." Beethoven was dedicated to the art of composing. It was his life force. In a letter to Ferdinand Ries in London dated December 22, 1822, Beethoven wrote, "I can compose, thank God, but do nothing else on earth."

Ludwig van Beethoven

December 9

"I was about eleven years old when my respected teacher and Beethoven's pupil, Carl Czerny, took me to see Beethoven. Already a longtime before, Czerny had told Beethoven about me and asked him to give me a hearing some day. However, Beethoven had such an aversion to infant prodigies that he persistently refused to see me. At last Czerny, indefatigable, persuaded him, so that, impatiently, Beethoven said: 'Well, bring the rascal to me, in God's name!'

It was about ten o'clock in the morning when we entered the two small rooms in the Schwarzpanierhaus in Vienna where Beethoven was living at the time, myself very shy, Czerny, kind and encouraging. Beethoven was sitting at a long, narrow table at the window, working. For a time, he scrutinized us grimly, exchanged a few hurried words with Czerny and remained silent when my good teacher called me to the piano.

The first thing I played was a short piece by Ferdinand Ries. When I had finished, Beethoven asked me whether I could play a fugue by Bach. I chose the fugue in C minor from the Well-Tempered Clavier. 'Could you also transpose this fugue at once into another key?' Beethoven asked me. (Beethoven himself was well known for his own transposition skill, having played the premier performance of his C Major Piano Concerto in another key, as the piano was not suitably in tune with the orchestra). Fortunately, I could. After the final chord, I looked up.

The Master's darkly glowing gaze was fixed upon me penetratingly. Yet suddenly, a benevolent smile broke up his gloomy features, Beethoven came quite close, bent over me, laid his hand on my head and repeatedly stroked my hair. 'Devil of a fellow!' he whispered, 'such a young rascal!' I suddenly plucked up courage. 'May I play the first movement of your C

Major Concerto?' When I had ended, Beethoven seized both my hands, kissed me on the forehead and said gently: 'Off with you! You're a happy fellow, for you'll give happiness and joy to many other people. There is nothing better or greater than that!'

This event in my life has remained, my greatest pride, the palladium of my whole artistic career. I speak of it only very rarely and only to my intimate friends."

Franz Liszt on his 1823 meeting with Beethoven

December 10

Beethoven composed *"Fur Elise"* in one day, April 27, 1810. He was 39 years old and at that time was giving piano lessons to Therese Malfatti. Much in love, Beethoven proposed marriage to her, but she refused. As best as we know, this was Beethoven's only proposal of marriage. Purportedly, Beethoven then poured out his emotion in composing this piece for her. Following her denial of his marriage proposal to Therese, Beethoven wrote to Baron Ignaz von Gleichenstein and said: "Therese's rejection of my marriage proposal plunged me from the heights of sublime ecstasy to the depths of despondency . . . It is therefore only in my own heart that I can again find sustenance and support: there is none to be had from the outside . . . Well, so be it! For you, poor Beethoven, there is to be no happiness from without. You must create everything you want in yourself; only in the Ideal World will you find friends." With Beethoven's handwriting notoriously poor, and this composition not published until after his death, the piece was copied numerous times and published as *"Fur (for) Elise."* Scholars know that Beethoven was never romantically involved with an Elise in this period of his life and believe that the composition was published with the wrong title. May we now recognize this very famous piano composition as *"For Therese."*

Ludwig van Beethoven

December 11

"Every day is lost in which we do not learn something useful. Man has no nobler or more valuable possession than time; therefore, never put off till tomorrow what you can do today."

Ludwig van Beethoven

December 12

"In February, 1827, Beethoven said to Gerhard von Breuning, "It was my wish to write many another thing. I wanted to compose the Tenth

Symphony, and then a Requiem as well, and even a piano method. This last I would have done in a way different from that in which others have written them."

Ludwig van Beethoven

December 13

In 1970, pianist Claudio Arrau wrote: "For me, Beethoven has always stood for the spirit of man victorious. His message of endless struggle concluding in the victory of renewal and spiritual rebirth, speaks to us and to young people today with a force that is particularly relevant to our times. In the sense that his life was an existential fight for survival, Beethoven is our contemporary. in the sense that he mastered both his life and his art to reach the ultimate heights of creation and transfiguration, he will last as long as man's spirit to prevail lasts on earth . . . In the end, Beethoven reached a mystical union with the Godhead, as it were, and on a higher plane of transcendence than almost anyone else in the history of Western Art."

Claudio Arrau on Beethoven

December 14

In a letter dated January 7, 1820, Beethoven wrote:
"I know no more sacred duty than to rear and educate a child."

Ludwig van Beethoven

December 15

Beethoven
"Shimmering Moonlight,
Shades of the Fifth,
Truly Beethoven had such a gift.
Of flowing his ink across the page,
With notes that live from age to age,
To give us great joy to hear or play,
I can feel him in this room today."

Nicholas Porter, age 10
Member of the Beethoven Society for Pianists

December 16

Birthday of Ludwig van Beethoven (1770-1827)
OP ED: "A Beethoven Music Odyssey"
The Emporia Gazette, September 30, 1992

"The man that hath no music in himself nor is not moved with concord of sweet sounds, is fit for treasons, stratagems and spoils. The motions of his spirit are dull as night, and his affections dark as erebus; let no man be trusted: mark the music." William Shakespeare *"The Merchant of Venice"*

"Like the astronauts of the space ship *"Endeavor,"* I went on a fantastic voyage this month. My space ship, entitled *"The Beethoven Society for Pianists,"* embarked upon its journey from Southern Illinois University at Carbondale. Commanded by Professor Donald Beattie, a superb musician and human being from Southern Illinois, and equipped with six nine-foot grand pianos furnished by the Baldwin Piano Company, it orbited the earth between Sept. 11 and 19, exploring the musical heaven of Ludwig van Beethoven (1770-1827), that Titan of composers. On board was a distinguished guest of honor, renowned pianist and teacher, Fernando Laires, and an international flight crew of some 70 pianists from North and South America, Europe and Asia; concert artists, faculty and students from many American universities, music schools and music centers of the world. The ground-control team and maintenance staff - the people who, along with Commander Beattie made the voyage possible - consisted of Carbondale's mayor, Southern Illinois administrators, faculty, students, staff and countless patrons, friends and citizens of the community and region. Their strong financial support, in-kind contributions, labor and gracious hospitality created a flawless system for the endeavor of the Beethoven Society."

Elaine Edwards
Music Professor Emeritus, Emporia State University (1930-)

December 17

OP ED: A Beethoven Music Odyssey (Part Two)

"The mission of the flight crew was to present performances that focused primarily on Beethoven's Nine Symphonies, 32 piano sonatas and selected chamber music. Some interesting compositions from our century were included throughout the week. Enthusiastic audiences numbering hundreds of adults and school children attended the concerts each day. Last spring, 1,000 children began to prepare for their part of the journey. While listening to Beethoven's music in art classes, they created pictures inspired by his music. A number were selected for presentation to the public at the close of the exploration. People were impressed with the imagination and originality of the pictures. The ground crew and maintenance staff kept the ship running smoothly and all personnel and equipment in top condition throughout the voyage."

Elaine Edwards

December 18

OP ED: A Beethoven Music Odyssey (Part Three)

"Why did Southern Illinois, a Midwestern university comprised of some 24,000 students and hundreds of faculty, embark on such a musical adventure? Because the dynamic commander, Beattie, convinced the entire crew, ground control and staff that such a voyage was a necessity, not a luxury, for the sake of all involved. And because Mayor Neil Dillard proclaimed that the City of Carbondale recognized the arts as an essential element in providing the opportunity to develop a quality urban environment. With the keen ability of a superior pilot, Beattie, along with distinguished guest artist, Stephan Moller, and crew, brought to the citizens of this picturesque region, exciting performances of Beethoven's music. This scholarly pilot and crew, sensitive to the climate of our time, knew in their hearts today's young people must hear and become acquainted with great music. Why? What lessons does the music of Beethoven teach children and adults? I believe such music reaches deeply into people's souls; it embraces and expresses all human emotions and passions. It enriches, inspires and transforms human life. It brings people to a higher plane of creative awareness and sensitivity. Above all, I believe great music triumphs over the adversities of life."

Elaine Edwards

December 19

OP ED: A Beethoven Music Odyssey (Part Four)

"Throughout his lifetime, Beethoven declared all men should be brothers. This seemingly impossible dream became reality during the week of the musical space ship's explorations. A conglomerate of people from various cultures and of many temperaments became a family with a mission. It was destiny that brought this family together. What will be the destiny of mankind? Can conflicting nationalities and countries be moved toward a brotherhood of nations through the power of great music? If people do not know great music, how can they be civilized? How can they survive and enjoy life? Let us Emporians build our musical space ship by supporting music and art, not just for ourselves, but for the preservation of a human culture that will embrace the right ideals and aspirations. If such is done, Confucius said, "we may see the appearance of a great nation." if we do not preserve and promote great music and art from the past, present and future, we may become a nation of barbarians."

Elaine Edwards

December 20

"I began writing these few thoughts the day after having heard the grand finale concert of the Beethoven Society's September 1992 Festival. I wanted to tell you that as I listened to he spellbinding performances of such eloquent and timeless musical statements of our 19th Century giant, I was somehow transported to another world of wholeness, rightness, balance and harmoniousness. In those two short hours, I became totally set apart from the turmoil of happenings, the sadness, and the brokenness of things around us! My heart and my soul were bathed with beauty, and I was refreshed, renewed, and invigorated! I am quite sure, also, that my thoughts and feelings were shared by all those around me."

Sister Alice Eugene Tighe
The Sisters of Loretto, Music Teacher (1915-2013)

December 21

"Beethoven Festival: From the Past into the Future"
Emporia Gazette, Emporia, KS. April 8 and 9 Weekend Edition, 1995
An Except of an Article by Mel Storm, Guest Reviewer

"Still familiar though the Symphony No. 5 may be in conventional performance, it is not easy to anticipate the effect of hearing it thundered from a forty-foot bank of grand pianos. As one who learned his childhood Beethoven from repeated playing of old Arturo Toscanini recordings and who, as a result, cannot to this day listen to any performance of Beethoven's symphonic music without automatically contrasting the sound of the NBC orchestra under Toscanini's baton, I went expecting novelty more than anything else. How mistaken I was! The primo secondo four-hand piano playing at five grand pianos in the Hugo Ulrich transcription, coupled with the Franz Liszt piano solo arrangement performed by visiting artist, Stephan Moller, creates an extraordinarily effective orchestra. This music is beautiful in its own right, particularly as performed by the Festival's artists. The impact of the massed sound can be astonishing. The unusual nature of the performance brings a new perspective to the familiar and enables us to perceive remembered beauty in new light."

December 22

Beethoven did take time from his work to socialize, entertain, and travel. In 1801, Beethoven said to Ferdinand Ries, "Am I not a true friend? Why do you conceal your necessities from me? No friend of mine must suffer so long as I have anything." Though some thought him a harsh man, he was sensitive and cared for others. To Frau Streicher in 1817, Beethoven said, "I would rather forget what I owe to myself than what I owe to others."

Ludwig van Beethoven

December 23

Beethoven was never seen in the street without a little notebook in which he jotted down his ideas of the moment. In conversation with Naegeli, Beethoven said, "I always have a picture in mind when composing." Beethoven brushed aside Czerny's suggestion that he composed for fame or to solve a problem: "Nonsense . . . What weighs on my heart must come out and that's why I've written." Speaking frankly to Naegeli during the turbulent years devoted to the "Mass in D," Beethoven said, "My chief object was to awaken, and deeply impress religious feelings on both singers and hearers." And on the manuscript of his "Mass in D," Opus 123, Beethoven inscribed "From the heart, may it go to the heart."

Ludwig van Beethoven

December 24

In a summer Beethoven study program in Switzerland, Wilhelm Kempff played all 32 piano sonatas for his class. From an article written by Madeleine Hsu for Clavier magazine, she quoted Kempff as saying: "The Voice of God is in Beethoven's music. Our century has been one of great inventions on the material plane; the spiritual has been relegated to the second plane. This period will be followed by a renovation of the spiritual . . . I deliver to you daily the message of Beethoven so that you can transmit it, you who came from such far-away countries as Germany, Canada, Estonia, France, Japan and Norway." Kempff continued by saying, "A young pianist can actually translate the character of Chopin's Sonatas, whereas the Beethoven Piano Sonata, Opus 111, is a world of philosophy; years of life, of maturity, are necessary. I undertake this last Beethoven Sonata with trembling."

Wilhelm Kempff
German pianist and teacher (1895-1991)

December 25

"Our spiritual work is one of service and love. We must always aspire to bring as much love and understanding to everyone with whom we come in contact. Begin to live a life of love and service in all you encounter and all you do. Be a living example of the precept of love. See all things as an expression of that creative love called God. Know that there is no need for judgment, for judgment is of the lower physical self, or ego, and what right do you have to judge others because they haven't learned a certain human lesson yet? Judgment often stems from fear. Fear is not living in the Godself. Rather, fear prompts judgments, prejudices, and petty ego stroking. Open yourself to the light of love in its purest form."

James Van Praagh
from "Talking to Heaven"

December 26

"Even though it might not be clear right now, your light on this earth is needed. There is no one else on earth like you because you are indeed unique. People need you! . . . Tell yourself how much you love and appreciate yourself for being alive and having the strength and courage to go through such an incredible adventure called life!"

James Van Praagh

December 27

"The aim and final end of all music should be none other
than the glory of God and the refreshment of the soul."

Johann Sebastian Bach

December 28

"I would teach children music, physics, and philosophy; but most importantly music, for the patterns in music and all the arts are the keys to learning. Music is a more potent instrument than any other for education as the movement of sound reaches the soul for the education of its virtue."

Plato
Greek Philosopher (approximate dates of 428-348 BC)

December 29

Birthday of Pablo Casals (1876-1973)
"Music will save the world."

Pablo Casals

December 30

"You must work - we must all work to make the world
worthy of its children."

Pablo Casals

December 31

In Paradise

"Getting late, getting tired, time to go,
Before I leave, heading home, I've got to tell you all,
What I've felt, what I've seen, what I know,
And how I've grown here, In Paradise.
Moonlight night, country road, take me home,
When I'm there, hand in hand, and with my family,
I'll recall, all of you and treasured time,
A humble moment, In Paradise.
Life is a precious gift, with voices help uplift,
Perhaps we'll not forget, Paradise,
Love is a precious thing, raise up and help to sing,
Through tears of joy it brings, Paradise.

Where I've been, who I've seen, what I've heard,
Ev'ryone, looking for, a special place like this,
Is it time to make the signs, that point the way,
So we might always, find Paradise.
Open hearts, open arms, open eyes,
Little steps, children seem to take the best of all,
Let them lead, you and me, don't be late,
They know the way home, to Paradise.
Life is a precious gift, with voices help uplift,
Perhaps we'll not forget, Paradise,
Love is a precious thing, raise up and help to sing,
Through tears of joy it brings, Paradise,
I thank you for the choice, to give the heart a voice,
And be as friends tonight, In Paradise."

Donald Beattie
c. 1993. Edition HAS Music Publishing Co.

Made in the USA
Middletown, DE
27 June 2023

33960355R00071